Mohamed Abou-El-Enein

Manufacturing Clinical-Grade Cell and Gene Therapy Products

Mohamed Abou-El-Enein

Manufacturing Clinical-Grade Cell and Gene Therapy Products

Economic Implications for Academic GMP Facilities

Südwestdeutscher Verlag für Hochschulschriften

Impressum / Imprint

Bibliografische Information der Deutschen Nationalbibliothek: Die Deutsche Nationalbibliothek verzeichnet diese Publikation in der Deutschen Nationalbibliografie; detaillierte bibliografische Daten sind im Internet über http://dnb.d-nb.de abrufbar.
Alle in diesem Buch genannten Marken und Produktnamen unterliegen warenzeichen-, marken- oder patentrechtlichem Schutz bzw. sind Warenzeichen oder eingetragene Warenzeichen der jeweiligen Inhaber. Die Wiedergabe von Marken, Produktnamen, Gebrauchsnamen, Handelsnamen, Warenbezeichnungen u.s.w. in diesem Werk berechtigt auch ohne besondere Kennzeichnung nicht zu der Annahme, dass solche Namen im Sinne der Warenzeichen- und Markenschutzgesetzgebung als frei zu betrachten wären und daher von jedermann benutzt werden dürften.

Bibliographic information published by the Deutsche Nationalbibliothek: The Deutsche Nationalbibliothek lists this publication in the Deutsche Nationalbibliografie; detailed bibliographic data are available in the Internet at http://dnb.d-nb.de.
Any brand names and product names mentioned in this book are subject to trademark, brand or patent protection and are trademarks or registered trademarks of their respective holders. The use of brand names, product names, common names, trade names, product descriptions etc. even without a particular marking in this works is in no way to be construed to mean that such names may be regarded as unrestricted in respect of trademark and brand protection legislation and could thus be used by anyone.

Coverbild / Cover image: www.ingimage.com

Verlag / Publisher:
Südwestdeutscher Verlag für Hochschulschriften
ist ein Imprint der / is a trademark of
OmniScriptum GmbH & Co. KG
Heinrich-Böcking-Str. 6-8, 66121 Saarbrücken, Deutschland / Germany
Email: info@svh-verlag.de

Herstellung: siehe letzte Seite /
Printed at: see last page
ISBN: 978-3-8381-3865-7

Zugl. / Approved by: Berlin, Charité, Diss., 2014

Copyright © 2014 OmniScriptum GmbH & Co. KG
Alle Rechte vorbehalten. / All rights reserved. Saarbrücken 2014

Table of Contents

1

List of Tables and Figures

Tables

Figures

List of Abbreviations

ADR	Average Daily Rate
AHR	Average Hourly Rate
ATMPs	Advanced Therapy Medicinal Products
CMV	Cytomegalovirus
CoGs	Cost of Goods
CTAT	Clean-Room Technology Assessment Technique
CTL	Cytotoxic T Lymphocytes
DQ	Design Qualification
EBV	Epstein-Barr-Virus
FACS	Fluorescence-Activated Cell Sorting
FS	Functional Specification
GMP	Good Manufacturing Practice
HSCs	Hematopoietic stem cells
HTA	Health Technology Assessment
HVAC	Heating, Ventilation, and Air Conditioning
InEK	Institut für das Entgeltsystem im Krankenhaus, Siegburg
IQ	Installation Qualification
LCL	Lymphoblastoid Cell Line
LN2	Liquid Nitrogen
MCB	Master Cell Bank
NUB	Neue Untersuchungs- und Behandlungsmethoden
OQ	Operational Qualification
PDM	Process Dependency Matrix
PEC	Process Evaluation Chart
QA	Quality Assurance
QC	Quality Control
QMS	Quality Management System
QP	Quality Planning
QPPV	Qualified Person for Pharmacovigilance
SIPOC	Suppliers, Inputs, Process, Outputs, and Customers
SOPs	Standard Operating Procedure
URS	User Requirements Specifications
WHO	World Health Organization

Abstract

Introduction: In addition to conventional drugs and biologicals, advanced therapy medicinal products (ATMP) represents a new class of medicinal products, which include - amongst others - somatic cell therapeutics. As the final product is intended for administration into humans, manufacturers of ATMPs are obligated to apply good manufacturing practice (GMP) standards within their processes. Reaching and maintaining such standards is cost intensive and requires sophisticated manufacturing facilities. As a result, academic researchers who are developing these novel therapeutic approaches are facing new technological and financial challenges. In order to have more commercially accessible therapies to patients and demonstrate efficient manufacturing technologies, we established the clean-room technology assessment technique (CTAT).

Methodology: CTAT is a two-level model: level one identifies operational (core) processes and measures their fixed costs; level two identifies production (supporting) processes and measures their variable costs. The model comprises several tools to measure and optimize performance of these processes. Manufacturing costs were itemized using adjusted micro-costing system. The model was tested prospectively in the GMP facility of Berlin-Brandenburg Center for Regenerative Therapies (BCRT), Berlin, Germany. CTAT assessment was validated in the GMP facility of the UC Davis, California, USA through retrospective analysis. To further analyze the benefits of the model, we compared its performance to the performance of a patient-based business model, which was used in the California facility.

Results: CTAT identified the activities in both GMP-facilities with strong correlation to the manufacturing process of ATMPs. Building best practice standards allowed for performance improvement and elimination of human errors. The model also demonstrated the unidirectional dependencies that may exist among the core GMP activities. The retrospective CTAT assessment of the California facility resulted in better allocation of their annual costs. The business model of the California facility failed to allocate 7% of their total annual costs which were considered sunk costs. The financial results of the CTAT model were used to build a fee structure in the Berlin Facility using an Average daily rate. In addition, a mathematical equation was developed to express the relation between Cost of Goods (COGs) and fee structure, taking into account the various cost drivers of manufacturing a cell-based product.

Conclusion: CTAT is not only considered a tool that provides CoGs estimates for advanced therapies, but also serves as a guideline for optimizing the operation of a GMP facility. The model has shown that production costs of ATMPs are mainly dependent on the method, duration and capacity of production. The model fulfilled its main purpose through the accurate estimation of product costs for two different GMP-grade ATMPs. Compared to CTAT model, conventional business models are suboptimal in evaluating the costs and performance of academic GMP facilities. Using CTAT may help in the translation of the current expensive GMP grade ATMPs into clinical practice.

Chapter 1: Introduction

1.1 Advanced Therapy Medicinal Products (ATMPs)

Advanced therapy medicinal products (ATMPs) is a new medicinal product category comprising gene, cell-based and tissue engineered therapies as defined in the European Regulations (1). Cell, gene and tissue therapies have been showing unprecedented opportunities in preventing and treating various diseases through replacing or repairing damaged tissue and/or cells (2). Important growth areas of high interest for these therapies include various transplantation settings e.g., generation of antigen-specific T-cells for immunotherapy (3, 4), or correction of genetic deficiencies in hematopoietic stem cells (5, 6), among others. The recent technological advances in manufacturing these products have further influenced their translational process into mainstream medical practice (7). Interestingly, ATMPs may have the potential to offer considerable commercial incentives once they are properly introduced into the pharmaceutical market. However, this business is still considered risky due to the absence of clear regulatory, commercialization and marketing strategies (8–10). Therefore, critical to the success of advanced therapy is not only the evaluation of clinical benefits but also the in-depth analysis of expenses associated with these products. Part of these expenses is the manufacturing cost which is mostly due to in process controls, product testing and laboratory expenses. Specifically, manufacturing of cell based products has to follow the principles of good manufacturing practice (GMP) as imposed by regulations (11) and guidelines (12). WHO defines GMP as a part of the quality assurance system which ensures that products are produced in a consistent manner and controlled to the quality standards appropriate to their intended use (13). This complex clean-room technology consists of several consecutive working steps, each of them contributing toward the aim of manufacturing a safe, potent and sterile product. As a result, the manufacturing process of cell-based products is lengthy, has built in variability and is costly.

1.2   Academic GMP Facilities

Many academic centers are now involved in clinical trials applying GMP-grade cellular, tissue or gene therapies (14, 15). It is therefore imperative for these centers to have access to manufacturing facilities providing clean-room technology. A GMP facility designed for an academic center is different from a pharmaceutical manufacturing laboratory, which is often used for the production of one specific product. In contrast, an academic GMP facility is usually designated as a "multi-use" facility since a wide variety of cellular products may be manufactured in an academic center GMP facility. This poses a challenge, since several cellular products may need to be manufactured simultaneously without interfering with each other. Therefore, separate manufacturing laboratories, at a minimum two laboratories, completely segregated from each other, should be available. After completed cell processing, product changeover, cleaning and residual product monitoring procedures need to be applied before the manufacturing of another product can be initiated. The necessary downtime during such changeover procedures is significant; a GMP facility with only one manufacturing lab may experience extended delays in manufacturing of products. If more than one manufacturing room is available, one room may be cleaned for the next product, while manufacturing may occur without interruption in the other room. A greater number of manufacturing laboratories therefore adds more flexibility; on the other hand, the operating costs of GMP facilities with too many manufacturing labs that sit idle for extended periods of time can become extraordinarily high. Good planning of a prospective GMP facility and a good estimate of future manufacturing demand versus operating costs is therefore a must.

Facing the reality of tight budgets and constrained resources in academic facilities, one of the main challenges for academia is to develop their own products without the need for outsourcing (16). Another key barrier is the lack of strong business expertise on how to control the Cost of Goods (CoGs) while maintaining a sustainable manufacturing process (17). On the other hand, large pharmaceutical companies have a well-developed understanding of how to manufacture new therapeutics at a commercial scale while maximizing revenue. Nevertheless, academia can benefit from exploring how pharmaceutical companies approach the introduction and manufacturing of new drug products. These companies have been employing business models in a closed innovation style as a representation of their business logic (18). Yet, at the same time, there exists insufficient disclosure and reporting of information by pharmaceutical companies on how these business strategies are applied and modified in practice (19). Hence, efforts to develop cell therapy products in academia call for developing tools to allocate and optimize production costs.

1.3 Manufacturing Costs of GMP-Grade ATMPs

The cost of operating a GMP facility is one of two cost components that are used to determine the overall manufacturing expenses of a product. It represents the value of such core tasks as initial planning, design, and construction, systems and equipment installation, hygienic monitoring, recruiting and training of staff and implementing quality management principles. These also represent the fixed manufacturing costs of a GMP-grade product. The other cost component is production costs which comprise the value of supporting tasks associated with production and directly involved in converting raw materials to finished products e.g. validation of production process, material and supplies acquisition and testing of final product, among others. These costs are the variable manufacturing costs that vary with the volume of production. Most of the operating and production tasks are interdependent and are therefore difficult to be assigned to only one of these two cost components. One of the major challenges is to recognize, analyze and dissolve this interdependency in order to accurately assess the economic impact of clean-room technology on manufacturing costs. This analysis will provide a better understanding of how a GMP facility operates and the expenses required to do so. At the same time, efforts should be made to optimize the GMP manufacturing process in order to cut back on expenses and eventually arrive at a reasonable price for these products.

1.4 Health Technology Assessment (HTA) and Reimbursement

Measuring the production costs of GMP-grade cell products is important since the process of bench-to-bedside translation of cellular therapies is influenced greatly by financial planning and investment (10). Understanding these costs helps in the pricing process of the product and answers several key questions, such as the cost effectiveness of the therapeutic product as compared to standard of care, commercial viability of these products and the market size that can be captured. Cost-effectiveness is one of the Health Technology Assessment (HTA) (20) tools that facilitate judgments on whether the benefits of these therapeutic interventions are sufficient to justify their high costs. Emphasizing the importance of HTA, new legislation became effective in Germany in 2011 stating that all new drugs that will enter the market should be subjected to a HTA with detailed costs of treatment (21). Additionally, achieving a reimbursable status for innovative therapies is a mean for the clinical use of these products in some countries such as Germany. The German reimbursement system offers incentives for hospitals that are willing to use innovative products to improve the health status of their patients. Hospitals can apply through a process called NUB (Neue Untersuchungs- und Behandlungsmethoden) (22) for the reimbursement of innovative technologies. If the application is approved by the InEK (Institut für das Entgeltsystem im Krankenhaus), the hospital will need to directly negotiate with the statutory health insurance to pay for these innovations. However, the success of this process requires the approval of health insurance providers which is mainly based on the accurate pricing of the products.

1.5 Novel Model for Measuring Costs and Optimizing Performance

"Given the magnitude of decisions depending on product cost, manufacturers usually estimate the costs within the framework of a business model. For pharmaceutical companies, the conventional models handle the therapy as a uniform product mass which is produced in industrial type GMP facilities on a large scale and then supplies a great number of patients (17, 23). This approach is suitable for allogeneic cellular therapy products. Other academic laboratories have developed patient-based business models, usually during a clinical trial phase, to handle autologous cellular products for a small cohort of patients (17, 23). Nevertheless, none of these modeling efforts where designed originally in accordance with GMP processes and no studies have addressed this subject before. Therefore, we developed the clean-room technology assessment technique "CTAT" as a two-level assessment model which focuses on the manufacturing process of GMP-grade cell, gene, and tissue therapies"(24). The first level of the CTAT model describes the core processes necessary to set up, operate and maintain a GMP facility, regardless of any production activities. The second level focuses solely on identifying and valuing the components of the production process of a GMP-grade product.

1.6   Aims

The aim of our study was to support the translational research and efficient manufacturing of the inherently expensive but highly promising ATMPs in academia. CTAT was employed to demonstrate for the first time how to practically determine the cost of a cell therapy product. Additionally, the model aimed to push the manufacturers to move from "average" performance to "best practice" levels which can reduce costs significantly. The development and application of the model required a full understanding of the different sectors of operating GMP facilities and manufacturing cellular products, such as facility equipment, quality management system, expansion methodologies and most importantly the instruments, reagents and supplies that are used during the process. Another aim was to demonstrate for the first time how to practically determine the cost of a cell therapy product using a mathematical equation based on the CTAT assessment.

We hypothesized that CTAT is a useful tool that can provide accurate CoGs estimates for advanced therapies. Additionally, it serves as an optimization tool for operating a GMP facility efficiently. CTAT was used for a prospective assessment of our newly constructed GMP facility based in Berlin, Germany. A retrospective CTAT assessment was also conducted using an existing GMP facility based at the University of California Davis, USA. The great strength of our model is the possibility to also integrate the inherent variability in each cellular product manufactured, such as duration of manufacturing and number of personnel. Further, we hypothesize that CTAT is superior compared to traditional business models in determining the cost structure of GMP facilities that manufacture cell-based products.

Therefore, we addressed the following questions / issues:
- Development of a novel cost modeling system – CTAT
- Implementing the model for analyzing the cost structure at the GMP unit of BCRT
- Identification of cost-driving processes within the manufacturing process to develop objective criteria for selecting the most efficient manufacturing technology
- Deviation of actual production levels in comparison with planned schedules due to human error
- Validation of the results by applying to another GMP unit in USA

Chapter 2: Methods

2.1 Study Overview

An initial review of the published literature was performed using standard databases and searching techniques. The result was poor and reflected the lack of information available on costs associated with operating GMP facilities and manufacturing cell-based products. The modeling effort was then conceived at the newly constructed GMP facility of the Berlin-Brandenburg Center for Regenerative Therapies (BCRT). The research center is located on the Charité University Medicine Campus in Berlin, Germany. The 400 m^2 space GMP facility includes: 1) Four manufacturing clean room suites (Class A in Class B) with material and personnel airlocks. 2) Analytical laboratory for quality control analyses and environmental monitoring efforts. 3) Secure documentation management area for control and storage of GMP documentation. 4) Support spaces for offices, storage and change rooms. The GMP facility is equipped with the necessary cell culture and purification equipment to produce experimental quantities of cell-based products for use in clinical trials. Prospective cost and performance analyses using the structured CTAT model were conducted at the same facility for GMP manufacturing of ATMPs.

A retrospective CTAT assessment was also conducted using an existing GMP facility based at the University of California Davis, USA. At the University of California Davis Medical Center, a 558 m^2 space within an existing building was required to accommodate the complete GMP facility with associated GMP Quality Control Testing Laboratory and GMP offices. Six rooms, separated from each other, serve as the core of the facility, and are the designated manufacturing laboratories. Two intermediate entry rooms and one common intermediate exit room allow personnel to enter and exit the manufacturing rooms while maintaining unidirectional flow of product, personnel and waste and complete separation of all manufacturing laboratories. Two gowning rooms and one common de-gowning room serve as the connecting rooms to the outside environment. Directed by an interlock system, which only allows opening of one door at a time, a gowning room, then an intermediate entry room, and finally a manufacturing laboratory may be entered. A diagram of the California facility can be seen in Figure 1. A layout of the Berlin facility can be seen in Figure 2. The relevant details of the two GMP facilities are provided in Table 1.

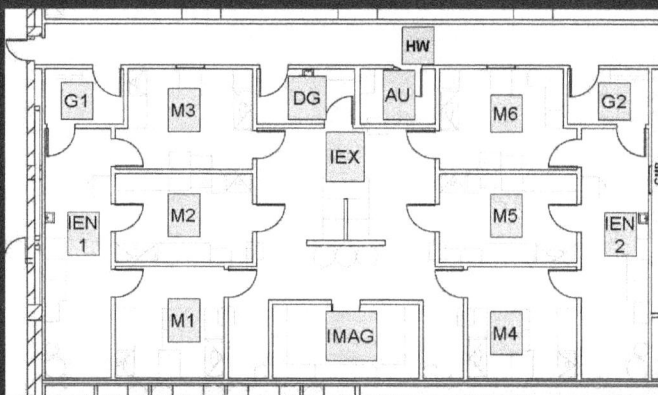

GMP Facility Stem Cell Program UC Davis

G1	
M3	DG AU M6 G2
IEX	
IEN 1 M2	M5 IEN 2
M1	IMAG M4

Legend:
G=Gowning Room
IEN=Intermediate Entry Room
IEX=Intermediate Exit Room

M=Manufacturing Room
IMAG=Imaging Room
AU=Autoclave Room
HW=Hallway

Figure 1: GMP facility diagram (University of California Davis – California, USA)

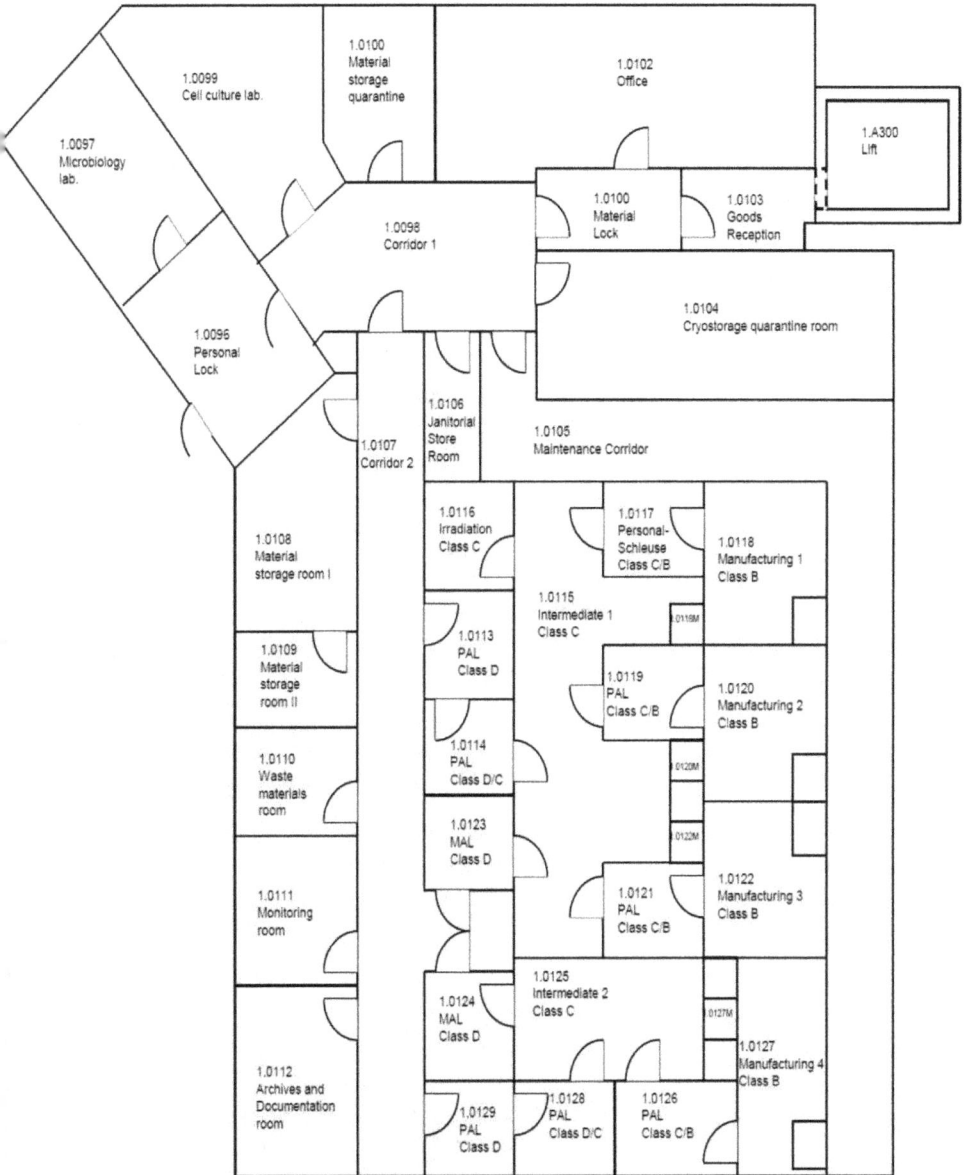

Figure 2: GMP facility diagram (Berlin-Brandenburg Center for Regenerative Therapies – Berlin, Germany)

	Berlin-Based GMP facility	California-Based GMP facility
Size	4,305 sq. ft. (400 m^2)	6,000 sq.ft. (558 m^2)
Structure	▪ 4 manufacturing labs (Class B) ▪ 2 intermediate labs (Class C) ▪ Cryostorage quarantine room (4 tanks for non-tested batches) ▪ Cryostorage release room (4 tanks for tested batches) ▪ Material storage quarantine room (for non-tested materials) ▪ Material storage room I (for materials tested and approved) ▪ Material storage room II (for materials tested and disapproved) ▪ Cell culture laboratory ▪ Analytical (microbiology) laboratory ▪ Monitoring room (central monitoring system) ▪ Waste materials room ▪ Archives and Documentation room ▪ Irradiation room ▪ GMP offices for director and personnel with computer equipment.	▪ 6 manufacturing labs (Class B, Class 10,000 US Standard) ▪ 3 intermediate labs (Class C, Class 100,000 US Standard) ▪ Associated GMP Quality Control Laboratory (not classified) ▪ Controlled temperature storage for incoming products (LN2, -80 deg C, -20 deg C, 4 deg C and room temperature) ▪ Sterilization using validated GMP autoclave in autoclave room. ▪ Validated, server based automated control and monitoring system in dedicated computer area ▪ Off-site storage for supplies and documents. ▪ GMP offices for director and personnel with computer equipment.
Staff	9 Personnel ranging from directors, quality control and quality assurance supervisors and personnel to production managers and personnel.	15 Personnel ranging from directors, quality control and quality assurance supervisors and personnel to production managers and personnel, fellows, graduate and undergraduate students.
Opened	6/2011	2/2010
Main equipment	Every manufacturing lab is equipped with one laminar flow cabinet and one centrifuge and two incubators. In addition an inverted microscope, fridge, a pipette aid and a set of micro-pipettors are also standard for each lab.	Every manufacturing lab is equipped with one 6-foot biosafety cabinet and one 4 foot biosafety cabinet and two dual chamber incubators. In addition, a tabletop centrifuge, a micro-centrifuge, an inverted microscope, a pipette aid and a set of micro-pipettors are also standard for each lab.
Specific equipment	-Autoclaves (intermediate labs and waste materials room) -Irradiation device (irradiation room) - Multicolor flowcytometer (cell culture laboratory) - CliniMACS (intermediate labs) for cell sorting -Controlled rate freezer for cryopreservation	-Ultra-centrifuge for gene therapy vector manufacturing -GMP grade FACS sorter in a bio-safety cabinet (manufacturing lab) -Controlled rate freezer, CliniMACS, fluorescent inverted microscope (intermediate exit lab) -Liquid nitrogen freezers, -80 deg C freezers, -20 deg C freezers, 4 deg C

	-Liquid nitrogen freezers, -80 deg C freezers, -20 deg C freezers, 4 deg C refrigerators	refrigerators (intermediate entry and exit labs)
Range of activities	Cell Manufacturing: a. Cell isolation / expansion / and storage (EBV specific T-effector cells, CMV Specific T-effector cells and Regulatory T-cells). b. Associated release testing: Viability, Sterility, Endotoxin, Mycoplasma c. Associated safety and potency testing	I-Cellular manufacturing: a. Cell culture / expansion / differentiation, master cell bank manufacturing and storage b. Gene transduction of primary cells (HSCs, etc.) for immediate patient infusions in a gene therapy setting c. Associated release testing: Viability, Sterility, Endotoxin, Mycoplasma d. Associated safety and potency testing II-Vector manufacturing: a. High titer lentiviral vector b. Retroviral vector c. Adeno-associated viral vector Associated release testing: Sterility, endotoxin, mycoplasma, tittering

Table 1: A description of the two GMP facilities participating in the study

2.2   Structure of the CTAT Model

"CTAT aims to identify all the physical parameters and components which proved to have the highest correlation in both performance and cost of a GMP manufacturing process. The model was designed as a "standardized structured shell" to be filled according to management objectives in relation to a specific GMP project. Due to the complicated nature of this process, where resources are not dedicated to only one activity in isolation, the model also aims to analyze and quantify the interdependency that exists between the various activities. For this specific reason, CTAT was designed as a two-level model: 1) *Level one* identifies the activities that are responsible for operating a GMP facility and that are referred to as core processes. The value of these activities represents the fixed manufacturing cost, also referred to as indirect cost. 2) *Level two* identifies the activities that are varied with the production procedures and are referred to as supporting processes. The value of these activities represents the variable manufacturing cost, also referred to as direct cost. The model integrates both performance optimization and financial estimation tools to ensure efficient delivery of the stated goals" (24).

2.3   Identifying and Categorizing GMP Manufacturing Activities

"The model starts with building a SIPOC (Supplier-Input-Process-Output-Customer) diagram. The diagram aims to identify all key activities in the GMP life cycle by listing their inputs, identifying their outcomes, and those who will benefit from each activity. The life cycle starts with setting up a GMP facility passing through all the operational and production processes and ends with having an applicable product which meets the required specifications. After obtaining this information, the next action is for the user to determine which activities fit into each level of the model. An interdependent activity with shared resources should be analyzed and broken down into finer details to determine how its individual resources can be categorized" (24).

2.4   Integrating Optimization Tools

"The model utilizes a Process Evaluation Chart (PEC), a quality improvement tool that helps to monitor the implementation of best practices standards that are established for the core and supporting processes e.g. least amount of resources or time each process should usually take. The performance of these processes can be strained by several factors including, but not limited to, utilization of a poor quality management system, ineffective use of personnel and failure to coordinate between individual activities. Therefore, comparing the actual performance of a core process to the PEC will help in clarifying potential problems where root cause analysis (RCA) (25) can be employed" (24).

"A simplified version of a Processes Dependency Matrix (PDM) (26) was also designed to further analyze the performance relation between the GMP core processes. The matrix shows the processes with dependencies on one another, either because of the flow of physical objects or flow of information. The matrix consists of two axes, the horizontal x-axis and the vertical y-axis. Each axis is labeled with the same activities that were identified in the SIPOC diagram. The matrix then depicts the dependencies between activities which can result from the flow of physical objects (e.g. materials) and/or flow of information (e.g. qualification reports). The extraction and exploitation of process dependencies is considered a part of the process evaluation which offers a better understanding of the overall GMP operations and can also highlight potential problems" (24).

2.5 Employing Cost Estimation and Analysis Tools

"Itemizing the costs of the GMP manufacturing process is achieved in the model using a micro-costing system (27). Personnel cost, another mixed cost component, has a unique approach in academic settings and specifically an academic GMP manufacturing environment. For instance, some of the personnel in an academic GMP facility have teaching responsibilities and also need to take on other non-GMP related projects; therefore, only their GMP-related working hours were factored in. For others, if their effort is 100%, their working hours are assumed to be 40 per week. The model then attempts to isolate personnel performing uninterrupted activities for management and maintenance of the facility from personnel carrying out the manufacturing procedures" (24).

"The cost data for GMP operations were collected in the model on an annual basis once the facility was up and running. The data were then presented as a percent of the total fixed manufacturing costs. There was no need for inflation adjustments which is usually required for studies evaluating costs accumulated over more than one year" (24). Information on cost estimations was gathered from different sources, (a) administrative and accounting data; financial reports and contracts between the engineering and enterprise departments as well as private companies responsible for setting up the GMP facility, (b) models; combining data from various sources involved in the process, and (c) experts' assessment of resource consumption that could not be obtained or was not possible to measure. "A payer perspective was adopted for the cost analysis. All costs were expressed in either euro or US dollar and refer to the year 2011. The cost data were then used by the Berlin facility to determine a fee structure for their operations and by the California facility to validate their existing fee structure"(24).

2.6 Examining the Business Model Performance in the UC Davis Facility

The GMP facility at UC Davis is a non-profit academic establishment. However, they planned their fee structure in a way that provides an average profit margin sufficient to cover rising costs of salaries, supplies, repairs, maintenance and unexpected equipment replacements when charging their customers. For prospective planning, the facility adopted a patient-based business model which handles each product as a single unit. They identified the key resources such as personnel, material, technology and equipment required to deliver the cell-based products to the targeted customer. The performance of their business model was assessed by comparing the prospective business plan to the actual performance of the facility by the end of the year. The cost data were presented as a percent of the total manufacturing costs (fixed and variable). For assessing the performance of the business model, we focused on the identification of the key resources in terms of quality and quantity, degree of efficiency in performing the various manufacturing activities and the clear understanding of the cost drivers influencing the manufacturing process.

2.7   Comparative Study: The Concept of CTAT vs. Business Models

Although no generally accepted definition of a business model exists, we aimed to demonstrate the most common elements and perspectives built into the concept of a business model and their difference to the CTAT model. Our comparative study was based mainly on our findings of 1) examining the business model performance in the California GMP facility, and 2) conducting a CTAT assessment on the two Berlin and California GMP facilities. During the comparison we also focused on a) evaluation of structural uncertainty, b) evaluation of measurement uncertainty, and c) availability of highly informative data.

2.8   Fee Structures: AHR vs. ADR

Both facilities determined a fee structure for their operations. The California facility ensures the availability of products for UC internal research purposes but also offers its services to external customers, whereas, the Berlin facility is currently concerned with producing cellular products for use in internal clinical studies only. At UC Davis, the facility established an average hourly rate (AHR) which was based on their business model when charging their costumer. This rate was then re-evaluated when the facility tested the CTAT model. The Berlin facility agreed upon an average daily rate (ADR) for estimating the price of their products. We analyzed and highlighted the difference between the fee structures of the Berlin and California GMP facilities.

2.9   Cytomegalovirus-Specific T-Cell Immunotherapy vs. Antiviral Therapy: A Cost Minimization Analysis

We performed a cost minimization study based on a hypothetical case management scenario of renal transplant recipients with high risk for CMV infection and disease. The aim of this study is to evaluate and compare the costs of GMP-grade CMV-specific T-cell therapy and antiviral therapy as prophylactic strategies for CMV disease in renal transplant recipients. The cost minimization study compares the two alternative therapies only in terms of costs and assumes the clinical outcomes to be equivalent (28). The standard prophylactic regimen for CMV disease in transplant recipients is obtained from the international consensus guideline initialized by the transplant society (29). Standard treatment was defined as 900 mg/day (two 450 mg tablets) oral Valganciclovir with treatment being initiated 10 days after transplant and lasting until 100 days post-transplant. Another prophylactic strategy was also evaluated which consists of 900 mg/day (two 450 mg tablets) oral Valganciclovir for 200 days (29). This dose is considered for patients with normal creatinine clearance (average of 120 mL/min). The drug was priced according to the wholesale acquisition price in Germany as described in the Red List (30). The total drug cost was calculated by multiplying the cumulative dose by the wholesale price. The costs of managing the adverse events that are associated with Valganciclovir were not taken into consideration (31). The cost required for I.V. infusion, including infusion equipment, syringe and needle for I.V. administration, the use of healthcare facilities and services were not included either. The second group are RTx recipients who will receive the adoptive immunotherapy with CMV-specific CTLs. The therapy involves the infusion of 3 doses (average of 1.7×10^7 total cell dose or $1 \times 10^7/m^2$ recipient body surface area) of CMV-specific T cells manufactured under GMP conditions. According to a single case study, the prescribed T cell dose was proven to be effective in a patient with severe CMV disease and resistance to antiviral therapy (32). CTAT was employed to calculate the costs of manufacturing a CMV-specific T cell line. The peptide-based approach using CMVpp65 and IE-1 peptide mixes was considered for the ex vivo generation of the cell line (33).

2.10 Epstein-Barr-Virus (EBV)-Specific Cytotoxic T-Lymphocytes (LCL technique VS. overlapping peptides technique)

Our GMP facility currently focuses on the development and manufacture of autologous Epstein-Barr-virus (EBV)-specific cytotoxic T-lymphocytes (CTLs) (4). To achieve Antigen-specific expansion of EBV-specific T cells, the Berlin laboratory has extensively utilized the expansion method which induces T-cell growth through a γ-irradiated autologous EBV-transformed lymphoblastoid cell lines (LCL). Another method is the expansion of T cells using mixtures of artificial overlapping peptide-pools. This method has already been established and used by the facility for the expansion of CMV-specific T cells using two main peptides (IE-1 and pp65) (33). However, the facility has recently adopted the same strategy for the expansion of EBV-specific T cells which is more cost efficient. CTAT was used to compare the financial impact of these two manufacturing techniques used for the production of EBV-specific T-cell lines.

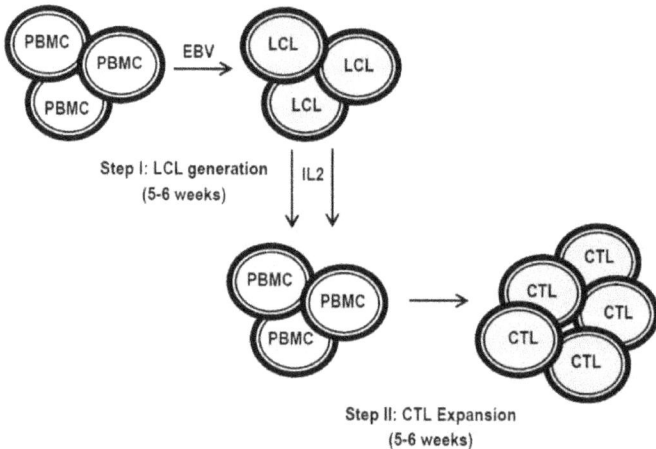

Figure 3: The manufacturing process of EBV-specific T-cells (LCL Technique). The manufacturing process of EBV-specific T-cells using the LCL technique requires an average of 11 weeks.

Chapter 3: Results

3.1 GMP Activities with Strong Correlation to the Manufacturing Process

The CTAT model produces a considerable amount of technical and financial details. The SIPOC diagram lists all the activities that proceed in a logical sequence and considered essential for implementing the clean-room technology and for starting up and operating a GMP facility within the specified standards (Table 2). The activities progress from site planning and construction, staff hiring, installation and testing of individual equipment components up to the implementation and testing of functional sub-systems and of the overall facility as a whole. Subsequently, planning of the production processes is carried out by addressing decisions on the acquisition, utilization and allocation of resources used to deliver the GMP-grade cellular product.

Suppliers	Inputs	Process	Outputs	Customers
Human resources **Project manager**	-Interviews -Candidates	**Recruiting and employing quality control and production Personnel**. Assign GMP tasks and provide sufficient training on knowledge necessary to perform those tasks.	Project team	**Project manager**
User	-Planning Meetings -Statement of Work (policy and strategy)	**Setting up quality management system (QMS):** quality planning(QP), quality control (QC) and quality assurance (QA)	QMS	**User/Future contractor**
User (Project manager and team)	-Planning meetings -Statement of work	**Prepare user requirements specifications** (URS) **and functional specifications** (FS) for the new GMP facility.	-URS	**User/Future contractor**

Contractor	Contract/URS/FS	**Site planning:** A set of drawings that identifies all mechanical, electrical and structural details.	Planning documentation	User
User	Risks/deviations/ changes control plans	**Risks, deviations (failures) and changes** to facilities, equipment, or processes that may have an impact on product quality must be reviewed, evaluated, controlled and documented.	-Management of risks, deviations and changes	**User/Contrac tor**
User/Contractor	DQ-plan/Site-planning documents	**Design qualification (DQ):** The first element of the qualification program that documents the validation of new facilities, systems or equipment.	DQ report	**User/Contrac tor**
Contractor	-Site-planning documents/ construction materials	**Site preparation:** Facility construction and installation of the HVAC system.	facility structure /HVAC system	**User**
Contractor	-Equipment specifications (USR/FS)	**Planning for equipment delivery:** A well-planned delivery schedule must be maintained to ensure all equipment arrives on time and according to specification.	Delivery schedule	**User**
Contractor	Delivery schedule	**Delivery and installation of equipment:** Execution of the delivery plan and the installation of equipment	Delivered/ installed equipment	**User**

User/Contractor	DQ-Report/ IQ-plan/ Installed equipment and facility services/	**Installation Qualification (IQ):** A documented demonstration that the equipment and facility services are installed as designed.	IQ report	User
User	-Supplies specifications -Purchase order	**Acquisition of medical grade gases:** The quantity and detailed specification of the gases to be purchased are described and a purchase order is prepared.	Medical grade gases (LN2 – CO2)	Vendor
User	-Garments specifications -Purchase order	**Acquisition of garments:** The quantity and detailed specification of the gowning to be purchased are described and a purchase order is prepared.	-Invoices -Garments	Vendor
User/Contractor	IQ-report/ OQ-Plan/ Ready installed and running equipment and facility	**Operation qualification (OQ):** Verification that the equipment functions according to designed specifications.	OQ report	User
Contractor	Equipment/ Manuals	**Operator's training:** Hands-on training where users learn procedural methods and proper operating techniques.	Training documentation	User

User **Disinfector**	-Hygienic plan -Detergents	**Cleaning and disinfection:** GMP compliant cleaning and disinfection are important parts in the preservation of the critical environment necessary for the manufacture of a sterile product.	Cleaning and disinfection report	**User**
User	Environmental monitoring plan -Contact and settle plats	**Environmental monitoring:** Provide information on the quality of the aseptic processing environment and identify potential routes of contamination.	Environmental monitoring report	**User**
User	GMP guidelines/manuals/ R&D documents	**Standard operating procedures (SOP):** Documentation for production and quality control.	SOPs	**User**
User	SOPs/ PQ-plan	**Performance qualification:** Verification that the equipment, when it operates, will consistently perform its intended function.	PQ report	**User**
User	Contracts/Audit plan	**Auditing of contract laboratories:** Evaluate the lab's compliance with GMP regulations and examine previous audit reports if present.	Contract labs Audit report	**Contract-Labs**
User	Production plan Validation plan/	**Media fill:** Validate the aseptic condition of a process using nutrient medium.	Validation report	**User**

User	Production plan Validation plan/	**Process validation:** Establishing by objective evidence that a process consistently produces a product meeting its predetermined specifications.	Validation report	User
User	Internal audit plan	**Internal Auditing:** To inspect the systems that will be used in any step of the manufacturing process, for compliance with regulations.	Internal audit report	User
Authorities	Manufacturing license application	**Regulatory auditing:** inspections of premises, products and QMS by the regulatory authorities.	-Regulatory audit report -Manufacturing license	User
Production department/Operator/Quality control/Qualified person/Contract-labs	Raw-material/SOPs/ Protocols/ Equipment/ Facility	**Production process:** Manufacturing of the product according to written procedures. 1-Reception of goods/raw material 2-Start production 3-Testing of final product 4-Release of product	Final product/Batch record/Release	Patient/Customer/ Clinic
Contractor	Maintenance-plan	**Maintenance:** Periodically performed to decrease the rate of wear of equipment and preserve their validated state.	Maintenance reports	User
Contractor	Requalification plan	**Requalification:** Periodically performed to maintain the qualified status	Requalification reports	User

| User | -Facility energy management plan

-Invoices for energy charges | **Facility energy management**: Efforts aiming to reduce the cost of energy used to run the facility without harming the ongoing processes. | Facility energy management report | **User** |

Table 2: SIPOC diagram describing the GMP life cycle. GMP life cycle starts with setting up a GMP facility (planning, construction and purchasing of equipment) passing through all the operational and production processes and ending with having an applicable product which meets all the required specifications. During this cycle some activities such as the personnel employment and qualification program, which consists of four types of qualifications: Design Qualification (DQ), Installation Qualifications (IQ), Operation Qualifications (OQ) and Performance Qualifications (PQ), are carried out once. Several other processes are carried out to maintain the status of the facility and are continued over the life expectancy of the facility such as maintenance, environmental monitoring, purchasing of material and supplies, natural gas supply, utility management, cleaning and disinfection, requalification and quality planning (shaded grey).

For the manufacturing of human cellular products or gene therapy products, specific consideration should be given to the physical arrangement of GMP-regulated facilities. The construction materials of clean-rooms should ensure ease of cleaning and sanitizing. Most of costs are incurred by the installation of the heating, ventilation, and air conditioning system (HVAC). Using straight line depreciation, knowing that the salvage value is zero and the average life span of the building component is 15 years, the accumulated depreciation of the Berlin facility after the first year is expected to be €108,000. Essential equipment such as the cell processing system (laminar flow cabinet / biosafety cabinet), cooling system (refrigerators and freezers), cell culturing system (incubators) and cryo-preservation system (controlled rate freezer, liquid nitrogen freezers and liquid nitrogen supply tanks) should already be considered in the planning phase. Similarly, the accumulated depreciation of the equipment's purchase, delivery and installation in the Berlin facility after the first year, with an average life span of 5 years, is expected to be €124,000.

The salaries of management personnel represent the value of activities that are merely operational and are independent of the production volume. The personnel expenses are the sum of all results after dividing the monthly salary of each employee by the working hours required (Table 3), which is estimated at €150,000/year. The process of testing equipment and systems is called qualification plan. An initial qualification process is performed; this process is followed by an annual requalification which costs €65,400/year. The Qualification plan is composed of: Design Qualification (DQ), Installation Qualification (IQ), Operational Qualification (OQ), and Performance Qualification (PQ). A cleaning and disinfection program as well as an environmental monitoring program for the facility must also be in place. These programs are monthly procedures that cost around €28,000/year and are required to maintain a microbiologically clean environment for the manufacturing processes. Environmental monitoring is accomplished by sampling air and surfaces at locations where significant activity or product exposure occurs as well as other locations more susceptible for contaminants in the clean-room. The process is usually done using two testing methods, 'settling plates', which are dishes containing appropriate culture media that are opened and exposed for a given time and then incubated to allow visible colonies to develop and be counted, and 'contact plates' which are agar plates that come into direct contact with the examined surface. Additionally, a thorough cleaning and disinfection of surfaces needs to be performed. Even if not in use, manufacturing rooms need to be cleaned on a monthly basis. These programs are usually carried out by trained personnel within the facility. In the Berlin facility, another twice per year monitoring process is performed by an external contractor to ensure optimal results.

Position	Salary/ Month	Hours/Week on T-Cell Production
Supervision	X1	H1 = 10 (39)
Qualified Person	X2	H2 = 10 (39)
Quality Assurance	X3	H3 = 39 (39)
Head of Production	X4	H4 = 39 (39)
Pharmacovigilance	X5	H5 = 5 (39)

Table 3: The administrative staff in Berlin GMP facility.

"The above-mentioned activities are part of the integrated requirements of a quality management system (QMS). A QMS usually contains three components: Quality planning (QP), Quality Control (QC), and Quality Assurance (QA). We considered the QP to include a) URS and FS b) Deviation and change control c) Risk management d) Inspections (Regulatory inspections, self-inspections and inspection of contract labs) e) Standard Operating Procedures (SOPs). QP requires maintaining thorough documentation for the entire GMP manufacturing process and is subjected to continuous updating and improvement. Therefore, this component is treated as a core process. The cost of performing the QP activities is merely based on personnel costs."(24) To estimate these costs, we multiplied the hourly pay rate for each member of the personnel by the number of hours spent performing these activities (this is extrapolated from the

PEC as will be discussed in section 3.4). As a result, an additional cost of €11,600/year is added to the total cost of operations. QA serves as the final authority, which assures that all quality control measures have been fulfilled, all prescribed parameters have been met and all tests on the final product have been performed. Thus, as a part of QA, validation of the production process and performing aseptic media fill controls are necessary before starting a production cycle (34). This structure is typically appropriate for the model to assign the quality-related activities to either the core (operation) or supporting (production) processes (Table 4).

	GMP Activities (manufacturing hierarchy)	CTAT Level-1	CTAT Level-2	Notes
1	Personnel employment	✓	✓	Interdependent task
2	**User requirement and functional specifications (URS – FS)**	✓		Quality planning
3	Site planning	✓		Capital asset
4	Design Qualification (DQ)	✓		Qualification program
5	Site preparation (facility construction)	✓		Capital asset
6	**Risks, Deviations and changes**	✓	✓	Quality planning
7	Equipment delivery and installation	✓		Capital asset
8	Installation Qualification (IQ)	✓		Qualification program
9	Natural gases (LN2 – CO2) supply	✓	✓	Interdependent task
10	Garments purchasing	✓	✓	Interdependent task
11	Operation Qualification (OQ)	✓		Qualification program
12	Cleaning and disinfection	✓		
13	Environmental monitoring	✓		
14	**Standard Operating Procedures**	✓	✓	Quality planning
15	Performance Qualification (PQ)	✓		Qualification program
16	**Contract laboratories auditing**	✓	✓	Quality planning
17	Media fill		✓	
18	Process validation		✓	
19	**Internal auditing**	✓	✓	Quality planning
20	**Regulatory auditing**	✓	✓	Quality planning
21	Manufacturing License		✓	
22	Start production		✓	
23	Maintenance (preventive/corrective)	✓	✓	Interdependent task
24	Requalification	✓		Qualification program
25	Utility consumption	✓	✓	Interdependent task

Table 4 The operational processes and the production processes in a GMP facility. The table lists the activities with strong correlation to the manufacturing process as extracted from the SIPOC and shows their relationship with the two levels of the CTAT model. The first level represents the core operational processes while the second level represents the supporting production processes. Other activities belong to the quality planning procedure and are interdependent. They are, however, treated and measured as a separate unit within the quality management system and considered as a core process.

"Other operational processes such as the annual maintenance of the facility and equipment, utility consumption and the acquisition of garments and technical gases have been shown to be interdependent (Table 4) and required further break down. In order to maintain the validated state of the facility and equipment, regular compensation for their "wearing out" must be applied via preventive and corrective maintenance. Preventive maintenance is scheduled at regular intervals, usually once a year, regardless the ongoing production process (core process). Conversely, corrective maintenance involves the repair or replacement of components which have failed or broken down due to the production cycle. Therefore, it is merely product dependent (supporting process)"(24). For utilities, the electric energy consumptions of HVAC and essential equipment were measured at rest (core process) by referring to the technical manuals. The HVAC system accounted for approximately 83% of the Berlin facility's total energy consumption and the rate of consumption is constant at rest and during activity (Table 5). "In case of product manufacturing, an additional rate of consumption according to different equipment performance was estimated at 20% for each manufacturing room" (24) (Table 6).

Source	percentage	Total Load/Year in MWh	Price in EUR/MWh	Total Cost
HVAC	83%	394	122.66	48.328 €
Equipment	7%	30	122.66	3.679 €
Others (lights, offices...etc.	10%	50	122.66	6.133 €
Total				58.140 €

Table 5: Total energy consumption in the Berlin GMP facility

Medical grade gases such as liquid nitrogen and carbon dioxide are required for running laboratory equipment. The Berlin based facility has eight cryo-tanks which are filled with LN2. The refilling is done every two weeks and uses around 1200 liters for each refill. The total cost of LN2 is €15,600/year. Another procedure, CO2 supply for cell incubators, costs around €6,000/year. Disposable office supplies, laboratory supplies that are not related to the manufacturing processes and communication services (phone lines and internet) cost €7,900/year.

Equipment	No.	Power values of equipment (W)	Expected energy usage at Rest			Expected energy usage during manufacturing		
			Base factor	Per single equipment per day (Wh)	For total equipment per day (Wh)	Use factor	Per single equipment per day (Wh)	For total equipment per day (Wh)
Laminar Flow Cabinet	1	420	100%	10080	10080	100%	10080	10080
Combi Fridge/Freezer -20°C	1	130	25%	780	780	30%	936	936
Incubator	2	30	0	0	0	50%	360	720
Microscope	1	n/a	n/a	n/a	n/a	n/a	n/a	n/a
Centrifuge	1	1400	0	0	0	5%	1680	1680
Tube Welding Set	1	n/a	n/a	n/a	n/a	n/a	n/a	n/a
Total	7				10860 Wh			13572 Wh

Table 6: **Expected energy usage for a single GMP manufacturing laboratory.** The table lists the power values of different equipment as presented in the technical manual in watt (W). The expected energy usage for each piece of equipment is calculated using a utilization factor. This factor represents the ratio of the time that a piece of equipment is in use during manufacturing to the total time that it could be in use at rest. The base factor is provided by the manufacturer in the technical manual since not all equipment is running at the same factors. For example, the Laminar flow cabinet has a base factor of 100% (switched on continuously for 24h a day). The use factor per day would also be 24/24 = 100% (the energy usage is not influenced by the manufacturing activities). Multiplying the 24 hours to the power value will give the expected energy usage per day in watt hours (Wh). On the other hand, the fridges and freezers have a base factor of 25%. Although they are switched on continuously, their energy usage at rest is equivalent to 6 hours of usage (collective estimation of times where energy usage reaches its peak). We then expected a slight increase of energy usage during manufacturing of 5%. Therefore, the use factor will become 30% which is equivalent to 7.2 hours. Multiplying the power value to the number of hours will then result in the expected energy usage during manufacturing per day. According to this calculation, the total energy usage is expected to increase 20% during manufacturing.

Cleanroom gowning is a basic component in a balanced cleanroom system. Gowning procedures are performed by the personnel in most of core processes and in all supporting processes. To separate between these two components, we identified the core processes requiring clean-room garments (Table 7). After adding 20 unplanned usages, a total of 156 usages of clean-room garments were estimated to be used by core operational processes per year. The basic stock was calculated to be 20 sets, which are the highest amount needed at once by one of these operations. And since the facility uses re-usable garments, a total of 156 sterilizations will be necessary by the end of each year. The price of buying 20 sets is €3,265. The average life span of a clean-room garment is 5 years, so the accumulated depreciation after the first year is expected to be €653. Adding €1,347, the cost of sterilization, the total cost is €2,000/Year.

Core process	Frequency of the process	Number of personnel	Duration of the process (in days)	Number of manufacturing laboratory	Total garment use per year
Clearings and Disinfection	Once per month	1	1	4 (class B)	48 sets
Environmental monitoring (internal)	Once per month	1	1	4(class B)	48 sets
Environmental monitoring (external)	Twice per year	1	1	4 (class B)	16 sets
Preventive Maintenance	Once per year	1	1	4 (class B)	4 sets
Requalification	Once per year	1	5	4 (class B)	20 sets
Additional unplanned usage					20 sets
Total usage					156 sets

Table 7: Planned cleanroom garment use. The table shows the Berlin-based GMP facility plan for garment usage to maintain the sterile conditions and the validated status in all of the four manufacturing laboratories. The plan represents the core processes which are performed regardless of the production activities. It explains the frequency of performing the process, the personnel carrying out the process and the duration of executing the process. Garments are then sterilized in separate laundry facilities according to written procedures. The plan also identifies the basic garment stock which is the maximum amount of garment used in a single process (20 sets). The Berlin-based facility has three processes that are carried out by external contracted companies and requires the use of clean-room garments. These are the external environmental monitoring program, the requalification and the preventive maintenance of the facility's systems and equipment.

"The different activities were aggregated into the two levels of the model as presented in Table 8. It is worth mentioning that, although differences can be found between the manufacturing of various products, the identified core and supporting processes are deemed necessary among all the GMP-grade products"(24).

CTAT	Level 1	Level 2
	Fixed costs (facility operation)	**Variable costs (production cycle)**
Personnel	-Wages and benefits for the directors and other administrative personnel	-Wages and benefits for the production and quality control personnel
Utilities	-Electricity and water usage (at rest) -Medical grade gases usage (at rest)	-Electricity and water usage (during activity) -Medical grade gases usage (during activity)
Maintenance	-Preventive maintenance (contracts)	-Corrective maintenance (prospective estimation)
Quality Management system	-Quality planning -Qualification program -Cleaning and disinfection -Environmental monitoring	-Media-fill -Process validation -Apply for a manufacturing authorization -Testing and release of final Product
Materials and supplies	-Clean-room garments -Office and laboratory supplies	-Clean-room garments -Raw-material and reagents

Table 8: The cost components of manufacturing a GMP-grade cell product. Since manufacturing activities require both, resources to operate and maintain the GMP facility and resources to produce a cell product, a CTAT assessment is designed as a two-level model. The first level allocates fixed costs that remain the same during the production period (do not include the depreciation of capital asset). The second level allocates variable costs which represent activities such as material purchasing, handling and processing that depend on the production.

3.2 Allocation of Fixed Cost to the GMP Manufacturing Process

The process of measuring the value of activities identified by the CTAT model after enumerating every input consumed by these activities can be seen in Table 9. According to a micro-costing estimation, the facility's annual operating expenses amount to €630,400 (Table 10). After deducting the capital costs, since they are covered by grants, the facility's annual operating expenses amount to €398,400. These expenses represent the fixed costs incurred by the facility each year which will then be incorporated into the final products.

Item	Cost Parameter	Cost Estimation
Personnel	Salaries of the personnel performing either operational duties or production activities	Personnel costs are calculated on the basis of the average rate of pay for specific personnel and their working hours, as required by the facility.
Utilities	Electricity and water: Cost of electricity and water consumption that result from the operational processes of the	Identify the energy consumable sources in the facility e.g. HVAC system and equipment. Cost of annual energy consumption = Load/Hours/Day (MWh) x Price (EUR/MWh) x

	facility (at rest) or during production.	No. of functioning Days/Year. Load is required amount of energy needed by system or equipment.
	Medical grade gases: Cost of LN2 and CO2 acquisition and refilling	The average purchasing price of LN2 or CO2 per liter
Maintenance	Preventive maintenance: Regular maintenance of the validated state of the facility's systems and equipment	Cost of preventive maintenance scheduled per year based on the price of the executing company.
	Corrective (unplanned) maintenance	Estimating costs of unplanned maintenance is based on projections and these costs are indirectly proportional to the frequency of the preventive maintenance.
Quality Management system	Quality planning: Salaries of personnel performing the QP procedure.	Calculate the hourly rate of personnel. Multiply by the number of hours spent performing QP activities. Calculate and sum the expected expenses on a yearly basis.
	Qualification program: Performing; DQ, IQ, OQ, and PQ for building, systems and equipment	Sum of costs of qualification tests per year based on the price of the executing company.
	Cleaning and disinfection of the clean-rooms	(In the case of external contractor: Cost of disinfector per square meter of area x total area) + costs of material and supplies
	Environmental monitoring: Sampling air and surfaces at locations with significant impact on the manufacturing process.	Sum of costs of testing plates: 'settling plates' and 'contact plates'. Depends on the surface area of production and frequency of sampling.
Materials and supplies	Buying re-usable clean-room garment (garment stock)	The largest amount of garment needed at once by one of the operations x their purchasing price.
	Office and laboratory supplies	The purchasing price of disposable supplies
	Materials and reagents for the production	The purchasing price of materials and reagents

Table 9: A micro-costing system for accurate manufacturing cost estimation. The built-in micro-costing system for the CTAT model enumerates the personnel hour, square feet of office space and supplies used. The system also represents the methods that were used for obtaining and measuring the costs of the consumed resources.

		Process	Cost/Year €	Cost/Day €	Cost/Day/Clean-Room Suite €
Capital Costs	01	Site planning & preparation	108,000	296.70	74.175
	02	Equipment installation & training	124,000	340.65	85.1625
Non-Capital Costs	03	Management personnel salaries	150,000	412.09	103.0225
	04	Qualification testing	65,400	179.67	44.9175
	05	Garments acquisition	2,000	5.50	1.375
	06	Cleaning and disinfection	20,850	57.28	14.32
	07	Environmental monitoring	6,350	17.45	4.3625
	08	Preventive maintenance	52,800	145.05	36.2625
	09	Facility energy management	59,900	164.57	41.1425
	10	Medical grade gases acquisition and other costs	29,500	81.04	20.26
	11	Quality Management System	11,600	31.86	7.965
Total		**Including capital costs**	**630,400**	**1,731.86**	**432.96**
		Excluding capital costs	**398,400**	**1,091.50**	**272.87**

Table 10: Annual expenses of the Berlin GMP facility

"The prospective cost analysis in the Berlin facility has resulted in 37% of the fixed cost as being related to the personnel salaries. Personnel salaries have in relation to the whole manufacturing process less relevant cost share, but for the fixed cost they are dominant. They represent the working time of administrative personnel that carry out managerial, quality-related and leadership responsibilities. Power, heating and water supply together have a share of 15% while the medical grade gases have a share of 16%. 13% of the cost is related to preventive maintenance of systems and equipment, followed by the validation program with 16%, cleaning and disinfection with 6%, environmental monitoring with 1.5%, as well as quality planning with a cost share of 3%. Materials and supplies were generally the least expensive components in the analysis, where 0.5% of the total fixed cost is related to clean-room gowning and 3% is related to office and consumable laboratory supplies" (24).

3.3 Retrospective CTAT Assessment of the California GMP Facility

"The CTAT model was then tested in the GMP facility at the University of California Davis, School of Medicine in order to strengthen the credibility of the model. As the facility had been conceived and made operational a year prior to the development of CTAT, GMP processes with associated fee structures had already been put in place using a business model. The retrospective cost analysis in the California facility was conducted using financial data that were originally collected for the fiscal year 2011 budget. The detailed information on the GMP manufacturing activities provided by the CTAT model enabled the facility to identify all their core processes with all of the incurred operating costs being accurately allocated. As expected, the highest share (30%) of the cost was for the personnel salaries. Surprisingly, utility consumption accounted for a relatively small share of costs (8%) compared to the smaller-sized Berlin facility. Additionally, with relatively low natural gas prices in the US, the share of costs of technical medical grade gas supply was 4%, therefore further reducing costs" (24).

"The California facility has negotiated special contracts for preventive maintenance and validation program resulting in a cost share of 8%, equally divided among them. The cleaning procedures have a cost share of 10% while implementing the environmental monitoring plan contributed 3% to the fixed costs. Addressing the quality planning activities as a separate unit has shown that the facility is spending a considerable amount of time and efforts implementing and conducting these measures. QP has a share of 12% which then influenced the facility to further improve the process. Materials and supplies have in total a high cost share of 25%. The distribution of fixed costs over core processes of both facilities is presented in Figure 3" (24).

Personnel	Directors (managerial duties)		37%
			30%
Utilities	Electricity and water		15%
		8%	
	Medical grade gases	5%	
		4%	
Maintenance	Preventive measures	13%	
		4%	
Quality Management system	Quality planning	4%	
		12%	
	Qualification program	16%	
		4%	
	Cleaning and disinfection	5%	
		10%	
	Environmental monitoring	2%	
		3%	
Materials and supplies	Clean-room garments	0.5%	
		5%	
	Office and laboratory supplies	2.5%	
		20%	

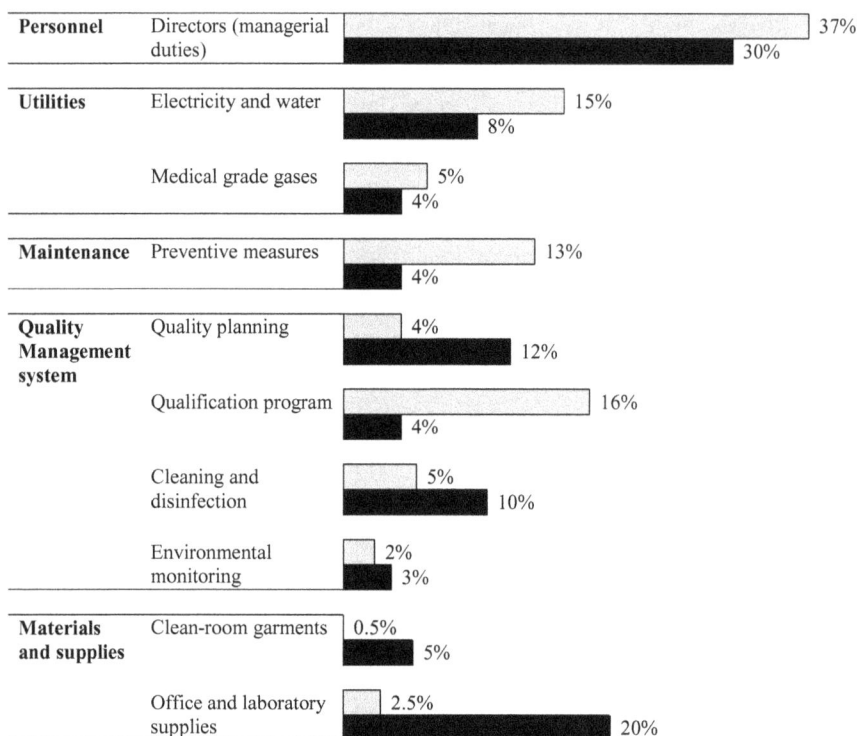

Figure 4: Expenses share of the Berlin facility (grey) and the California facility (black). Estimated operating expenses of the Berlin facility are presented as percentage for the years 2011-2012. The actual operating expenses of the California facility are presented as percentage for the years 2010-2011. The resources consumed were identified and their value was measured using a micro-costing system. For the retrospective CTAT assessment in the California facility, financial data traced for the fiscal year 2011 budget were completely allocated to the identified core and supporting processes.

3.3   Setting up a Fee Structure in an Academic GMP Facility

"The identification of the annual fixed costs for both facilities was crucial in setting a fee structure for their operations. As the California facility had been operational a year prior to the application of CTAT, GMP processes with associated fee structures had already been put in place using traditional business model. UC Davis decided that an AHR for manufacturing GMP-grade cell products would be best for their customer base. This resulted in a fee of 475 USD (approximately 375 EUR) per hour which was also verified and approved by the UC Davis Rates Committee. On the other hand, the Berlin facility established an ADR which was approved at 270 EUR for each single manufacturing laboratory. Multiplying this rate by the total days required for manufacturing a product will give the exact fixed cost portion incorporated into the final product. Adding the variable costs will then determine the final price of the product" (24).

3.4   CTAT Helps to Move from "Average" Performance to "Best Practice" Levels

"In the Berlin facility, the best use of resources has been identified for all GMP activities, which involve mainly manpower. As part of the prospective data collection for this evaluation, number of personnel, length of time, and supplies necessary to perform the activities were estimated based on expert opinions (Table 11). The facility then should comply with these standards during performance. The retrospective CTAT assessment of the California facility also benefited from the PEC tool. For instance, we were able to identify activities that took too long (purchasing of gowning and supplies), involved too many man-hours (e.g. quality planning), and included redundant or unnecessary steps (e.g. cleaning and disinfection). Supporting processes that are involved in the product manufacturing were also subjected to frequent delays (e.g. occasional lack of personnel, unexpected equipment malfunction or purchased materials could not meet the GMP standards)" (24).

	Process	Time	People	Materials	Space
Once in a lifetime processes (improvement opportunities are limited to prospective planning)					
1	Site planning	6 months	10 (8xTechnical planning department of the contractor/Head of production/Head of Quality control)	Documents Office supplies	9 Offices
2	Site preparation	6 months	9 (8xTechnical planning department of the contractor/Project planner[1])	Tools Documents Office supplies	9 Offices
Once in a lifetime processes, repeated under certain conditions[2] (improvement opportunities are present)					
3	Management staff employment	12 days	2 (Qualified person/HR manager /Project planner)	Documents Office supplies	3 Offices Meeting Room
4	Equipment delivery Equipment	12 days 8-9	2 (Contractor/Project planner)	Vehicles Tools	All rooms in the facility

#	Process	Duration	Personnel	Resources	Rooms
	installation	weeks		Documents	Elevator
5	Operator's training[3]	2 weeks	7 (Contractor/3x Production/3x Quality control)	Equipment Documents	All rooms in the facility
6	Design Qualification	2 weeks	3 (Contractor/Head of production/Head of Quality control)	Documents Office supplies	2 Offices
7	Installation Qualification	1 month	2 (Head of production/Head of Quality control)	Documents Office supplies	4 Clean-Rooms 2 Quality Control Labs 3Storage Rooms 2 LN2-Rooms 1 Office
8	Operation Qualification	3 month	2 (Head of production/Head of Quality control)	Documents Office supplies	4 Clean rooms 2 Quality Control Labs 3Storage Rooms 2 LN2-Rooms 1 Office
9	Performance Qualification	6 weeks	2 (Head of production/Head of Quality control)	Documents Office supplies	4 Clean rooms 2 Quality Control Labs 3Storage Rooms 2 LN2-Rooms 1 Office
Regularly performed Processes (improvement opportunities are present)					
10	Garments acquisition Garments sterilization	1 weeks 1 day/week	2 (Head of production/ Purchasing Department[4])	Documents Office supplies	2 Offices
11	Cleaning and disinfection	1 day/ month	2 (Head of production/ Disinfector[5])	Documents Detergents Gowning	4 Clean-Rooms 1 Storage Room 1 Office
12	Environmental monitoring	2 days/ month	2 (Head of Quality Control/Head of production)	Documents Consumables Gowning	4 Clean-Rooms 1 Storage Room 1 Office

13	Requalification	1 weeks/ year	2 (Head of Quality Control/Head of production)	Tools Documents Office supplies	4 Clean rooms 2 Quality Control Labs 3 Storage Rooms 2 LN2-Rooms 1 Office
14	Preventive maintenance	1 weeks/ year	3 (Contractor/Head of Quality Control/Head of production)	Tools Spare-parts Documents Office supplies	4 Clean rooms 2 Quality Control Labs 3 Storage Rooms 2 LN2-Rooms 1 Office
15	Facility energy management	3 days/ year	2 (Head of Quality Control/Head of production)	Documents Office supplies	1 Office
16	Medical grade gases Acquisition Refill	2 days 1h/week	2 (Head of production/ Purchasing Department)	Documents Office supplies	2 Offices
Quality Planning (improvement opportunities are present)					
17	User requirement and functional specifications	7 days	3 (Qualified person/Head of Quality Control/Head of production)	Documents Office supplies	2 Offices
18	Risks, Deviations and changes	4h/week	6 (Qualified person/QPPV/ Head of Quality Control/Head of production/ Contractor/Project Planner)	Documents Office supplies	5 Offices
19	Standard Operating Procedures	8h/week	7 (Qualified person/3x Production/3x Quality control)	Documents Office Supply	2 Offices
20	Contract laboratories auditing	12 days	2 (Head of Quality Control/Head of production)	Documents	Contract Labs 1 Office
21	Internal auditing	5 days/year	8 (Qualified person/QPPV/3x Production/3x Quality	Documents	Facility 4 Offices

			control)			
22	Regulatory auditing	3 days	8 (Qualified person/QPPV/3x Production/3x Quality control)	Documents	Facility 3 Offices	

Table 11: Process evaluation chart for the GMP activities. This step creates best practice standards that are used to manage a project to meet objectives. The chart discusses the best use of time, people and materials to execute each process based on expert opinion.

1-Project planner: The Project Planner is an employee in the Charité University Medicine who partners with the GMP team to support, analyze and report progress of the project against schedules.

2-Repeated processes under certain conditions: These processes can be repeated if new personnel are employed or new equipment is purchased.

3- Operator's training: The process involves all the GMP personnel, including the production and quality control staff. Therefore, we added the working hours of these personnel to the total cost of the process (since production and quality control personnel are an enabling process related component).

4-Purchasing department: All purchases and requisitions for quotation should be made with the authority of the Charité University Medicine purchasing department.

5-Disinfector: The cleaning and disinfection process is carried out by a qualified disinfector. The disinfector is charged per square meter of area.

"Every purchasing or usage activity during the GMP manufacturing process has basic procedures that universally apply to various facilities. For example, there are events during a clean-room garment purchasing cycle that consume time as shown in Figure 4. Some add value, such as on time receiving and inspecting the garments. Some are non-value adding and delay time, such as the failure of suppliers to deliver the requested garments on time, or delays in processing of purchasing documents. Mapping the flow and tracking time for each of the events provides a basis for building best practice standards. The percentage of non-value adding time which may constitute up to 90 percent of total time can be reduced or even eliminated. It can be concluded from the process dependency matrix that such delay can affect the performance of other related processes" (24).

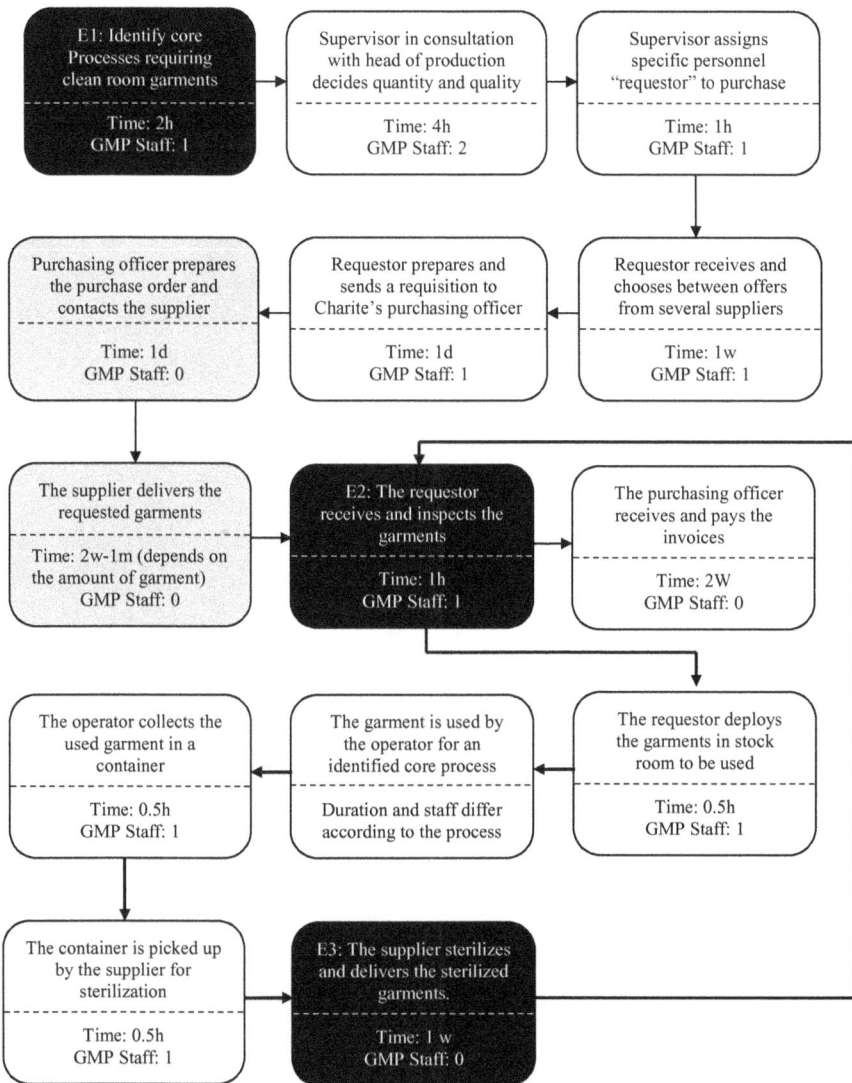

Figure 5: The Purchasing cycle of clean-room garment. The diagram depicts the flow of events that are required for 1) purchasing clean-room garment (the cycle starts with E1 and ends with E2) and 2) Using and sterilizing the purchased garment (the cycle starts with E2 and ends with E3). During these cycles there are some events that can add value and others that are non-value adding. Example of non-value adding events are those which cause delays in the chain of procedures and can be improved (grey). The facility established best practice standards which represent the best case scenario for performing these events and any deviation from those standards should be avoided.

"Referring to the PDM, it was observed that the flow of GMP information and physical objects is unidirectional, as the dependency relationships are located on just one side of the diagonal. Figure 5 represents a simple PDM for the core activities of a GMP manufacturing process. For example, examining the first row we note that activity No. 10 (gowning acquisition) and activity No. 12 (operator training) depends on activity No. 1 (personnel employment).Overall, human error is still the most prevalent factor that may introduce problems and increase the level of uncertainty" (24).

Figure 6 — GMP Processes Dependency Matrix

	1	2	3	4	5	6	7	8	9	10	11	12	13	14	15	16	17	18	19	20	21	22
1	■									1→10		1→12										
2		■	2→3	2→4	2→5	2→6	2→7	2→8	2→9		2→11					2→16						
3			■	3→4	3→5	3→6	3→7	3→8			3→11					3→16				3→20		
4				■		4→6		4→8										4→18	4→19			
5					■		5→7	5→8														5→22
6						■		6→8			6→11			6→14	6→15	6→16		6→18	6→19	6→20	6→21	
7							■	7→8	7→9			7→12										7→22
8								■			8→11							8→18	8→19			
9									■		9→11				9→15							9→22
10										■			10→13	10→14		10→16				10→20	10→21	
11											■		11→13		11→15	11→16		11→18	11→19			
12												■			12→15	12→16		12→18	12→19			
13													■	13→14								
14														■		14→16		14→18	14→19			
15															■	15→16		15→18	15→19	15→20	15→21	
16																■		16→18	16→19	16→20		
17																	■		17→19			
18																		■	18→19			
19																			■			
20																				■	20→21	
21																					■	
22																						■

Figure 6: GMP Processes Dependency Matrix. The matrix depicts the dependencies that exist between activities which were listed in the SIPOC diagram and required for setting up and operating the GMP facility. 1-Staff employment, 2-User Requirement Specification (URS), Functional Specification(FS), 3-Site planning, 4-Design Qualification (DQ), 5-Site preparation, 6-Risks, Deviations & change management, 7-Equipment delivery and installation, 8-Instalation Qualification (IQ), 9-Medical grade gases acquisition, 10-Gowning acquisition, 11-Operation Qualification (OQ), 12-Operators training, 13- Cleaning disinfection, 14-Environmental monitoring, 15-Standard Operating Procedures (SOPs), 16-Performance Qualification (PQ), 17- Contract laboratories auditing, 18-Internal auditing, 19-Regulatory auditing, 20-Preventive maintenance, 21-Requalification, 22-Utility consumption (Facility energy management). Process dependencies can be due the flow of physical objects or flow of information. Process "X" →Process "Y": This means process Y receive physical object and/or information from process X.

3.5   Cross-Subsidization: Improper Assignment of Costs by Business Models

"Before adopting the CTAT model, the California facility has already used a patient-based business model for prospective planning. They considered in their business model human assets (personnel time and effort) and physical assets (utilities and materials). Additionally, they identified three processes (qualification program, maintenance and environmental monitoring) required to maintain the GMP status of the facility. The facility management did not focus on the proportion of manufacturing costs that are strictly fixed or variable. However, they considered all the key resources and activities mentioned above as the base for calculating their cost structure. Materials, reagents and release testing specific for each product were regarded as additional costs. The facility then attempted to measure their cash flow projections. In total, the share of annual expenses was expected to be 80% of the total revenue for the reference years 2010/2011 (since the best possible profit margin was expected to be 20%). The highest share with 31% was expected to be the personnel costs, followed up by the key GMP processes with 19%. Utility costs (electricity, water, gas) were expected to be 16%. Finally, materials and supplies (gowning, consumable laboratory and office supplies) accounted for 14% of the total expenses"(24).

"The actual expenses of the facility were then allocated after being analyzed for the retrospective CTAT assessment (Figure 6). The actual expenses made up 92% of gross revenue, including wages and benefits at 35.7%, GMP processes at 17.8%, utilities at 10.2% and materials and supplies at 21.3%. Therefore, 7% of costs were considered sunk costs and couldn't be allocated within the business model forecasts. However, it was easy to conclude that these sunk costs are part of variable costs of the manufacturing process (Table 12). Accordingly, the profit was 12% less than expected which can be considered a type of bias. This is due to the sunk costs that weren't charged to the customers and the significant uncertainty between the actual financial performance and the projections"(24).

		31%
Personnel
35.7%

Utility — 16%
10.2%

GMP Processes — 19%
17.8%

Materials — 14%
21.3%

Sunk Costs — 7%

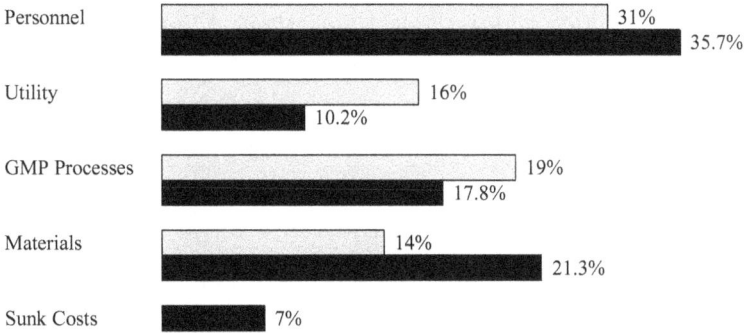

Figure 7: California facility's projected expenses share (grey) vs. actual expenses share (black). Estimated operating expenses of the California facility are presented as percentage for the years 2010-2011 (grey) and compared to the actual operating expenses for the same year (black). The actual expenses were allocated after being analyzed for the retrospective CTAT assessment. The presence of sunk costs suggests the inaccuracy of the business model in the prospective identification of all the activities with strong correlation to the GMP manufacturing process.

	Resources	Process
1	Personnel working hours	Personnel performing quality control measures, internal auditing or additional cleaning procedures
2	Utility consumption (electricity and medical grade gases)	Usage of incubators and liquid nitrogen freezers during manufacturing
3	Equipment spare parts	Corrective maintenance and repair of equipment
4	Cleaning reagents	Cleaning and residual product monitoring procedures
5	Materials, office and laboratory supplies	Gowning, documentation and several other processes

Table 12: The allocation of the sunk costs among the multiple processes. The sunk costs were estimated at 7% of the total facility revenue for the years 2010-2011. Analyzing these costs retrospectively showed several resources to be involved. These unrecoverable costs were found to be part of the total variable expenses of manufacturing several products throughout the year (excluding the raw-materials, reagents and release testing specific for each product). They represent 1) excess personnel working hours, 2) excess utility consumption, 3) unplanned corrective maintenance and repair, 5) cleaning and residual product monitoring procedures after each production cycle, 6) excess office and laboratory supplies and gowning.

3.6   What is the Price Tag of a GMP-Grade ATMP?

The relation between using a fee structure and estimating product cost within the CTAT model is presented in a mathematical equation (Figure 7). We then demonstrated how the equation was employed to estimate the cost of two different products using the two fee structures (24).

$$\sum_{i=1}^{2} Manufacturing\ cost\ Product_i = \sum_{i=1}^{n} operating\ cost\ Facility_{i_{fix}} \cdot time + \sum_{i=1}^{n} production\ cost\ Product_{i_{var}}$$

Figure 8: The mathematical basis of the CTAT model. Where n is the number of cost components, time is the duration of the product manufacturing, FIX is the fixed cost category (level 1) which is represented by the fee structure of the facility and VAR is the variable cost category (level 2).

"For the California facility, manufacturing of autologous hematopoietic stem and progenitor cell gene modified with a lentiviral vector was chosen as an example (35). For these products, a three-step manufacturing process is required; 1) establishing a master cell bank for lentiviral vector manufacturing incl. release testing and storage, 2a) production of GMP grade plasmid for lentiviral vector manufacturing, 2b) clinical grade lentiviral vector manufacturing incl. release testing and storage and 3) GMP grade autologous CD34+ cell transductions incl. release testing. The facility used the model to estimate the variable costs of each manufacturing step (Tables 13, 14). The costs of establishing the master cell bank were estimated at $36,292. The fully tested master cell bank can be used for multiple gene therapy vector manufacturing. Enough lentiviral vectors were manufactured for a predicted production capacity of 10 gene therapy products. The plasmid manufacturing and testing were outsourced and cost $29,000 (14,000 for production and 15,000 for certification). Total costs for 10 GMP grade lentiviral vectors including plasmid manufacturing and testing were estimated at $84,917. Finally, costs per autologous CD34+ cell transduction culture were estimated at $34,063. The facility calculated the fixed GMP costs for each step using their approved AHR. It was determined that the process will need 18 hours for master cell bank production, 22 hours for vector production and 10 hours for each CD34+ cell transduction under GMP conditions. Additional fixed costs were estimated to cover the costs of master cell bank storage under GMP conditions for one year. Similar storage costs including two stability tests per 6 months were also added to the lentiviral vector`s fixed costs. The final price for a single transduced hematopoietic stem cell product came to $54,000 (approximately €44,500) (Figure 7)" (24).

Variable Resources (CTAT Level 2)	Description	Variable costs ($)		
		master cell bank (MCB)	lentiviral vector (LV)	CD34+ cell transductions (CT)
1. Materials and supplies	Media and supplements & Plasticware	8,814	6,844	6,844
	Transfection reagents	N/A	9,500	N/A
	Sterilized purification columns	N/A	8,500	N/A
	Apheresis Product (mobilized peripheral blood stem cells)	N/A	N/A	8,000
	Reagents for the CliniMacs	N/A	N/A	6,000
	GMP grade cytokines	N/A	N/A	3,000
	Garments (240 sets)	1,838	1,838	1,838
2. Personnel	Production personnel	9,640	9,158	5,784
3. Utilities	Electricity, water & medical grade gases	1,000	1,250	550
4. Maintenance	Corrective maintenance			
5. Quality Management system	Media-fill & process validation	15,000	18,827	2,047
	Batch release testing (Testing for sterility, mycoplasma, endotoxin and other items required by regulations)			
Total		36,292	55,917	34,063

Table 13: The variable costs of manufacturing GMP-grade transduced hematopoietic stem cell products. The variable resources of the manufacturing process were identified according to the second level of the CTAT model. The estimated variables costs of the master cell bank and lentiviral vector production are supposed to be depreciated over 10 hematopoietic stem cell products. The costs of GMP grade plasmid production were not included in this table since the process is being outsourced by the facility. However, these costs are supposed to be depreciated over 10 products and added to the final product costs.

	Unit fixed costs ($)	Unit variable cost ($)	Total unit cost ($)
Master cell bank	1,170.7	3,629.2	4,799.9
Lentiviral vector	2,043	5,591.7	7,634.7
Cell transductions	4,750	34,063	38,813
Total	7,963.7 (15.5%)	43,283.9 (84.5%)	51,247.6
Outsourced (Plasmid)	2,900		2,900
Total unit cost			54,147.6

Table 14: The fixed and variable cost shares in the manufacturing of a single lentiviral vector transduced autologous hematopoietic stem cell product. The fixed costs represent 15.5% while the variable costs represent 85% of the total manufacturing costs. The high percentage of variable costs is due to the complex steps of the manufacturing process.

$$\sum_{i=1}^{2} Manufacturing\ costMCB = [(\$475 \times 18) + \$2,857] + \$36,292 = \$47,999$$

a) **The total manufacturing costs of a GMP-grade master cell bank (MCB).** Additional costs of storage were estimated at $2,857 and added to the fixed costs. The duration of the master cell bank manufacturing under GMP conditions was estimated at 18 hours which was then multiplied by the AHR. The total costs of a single MCB manufacturing were then depreciated over 10 products.

$$\sum_{i=10}^{2} Manufacturing\ costLV = [(\$475 \times 22) + \$9,980] + \$55,917 = \$76,347$$

b) **The total manufacturing costs of 10 GMP-grade lentiviral vectors (LV).** Additional costs for storage and stability testing were estimated at $9,980 and added to the fixed costs. The duration of the lentiviral vectors manufacturing under GMP conditions was estimated at 22 hours which was then multiplied by the AHR. The total costs of lentiviral vectors manufacturing were then depreciated over 10 products.

$$\sum_{i=1}^{2} Manufacturing\ costCT = (\$475 \times 10) + \$34,063 = \$38,813$$

c) **The total manufacturing costs of a single GMP-grade CD34+ cell transduction (CT).** The duration of the CD34+ cell transduction under GMP conditions was estimated at 10 hours which was then multiplied by the AHR.

$$\sum_{i=1}^{3} Manufacturing\ costHSC = \$4.799.9 + (\$7.634.7 + \$2,900) + \$38,813 = \$54,147.6$$

d) **The total manufacturing costs of a single lentiviral vector transduced autologous hematopoietic stem cell (HSC) product.**

Figure 9 (A-D): The calculation of the manufacturing costs of a single lentiviral vector transduced autologous hematopoietic stem cell (HSC) product. The total manufacturing costs are the sum of the a) depreciated expenses of manufacturing the master cell bank over 10 products, b) the depreciated expenses of manufacturing the lentiviral vectors and outsourcing plasmid production over 10 products, and c) the total costs of a single CD34+ cell transduction

3.7 CMV-Specific T-Cell Immunotherapy is an Economically Relevant Strategy

We estimated the GMP fixed costs for a single CMV-specific peptide stimulated T cell line at €5,670, knowing that manufacturing of a single T cell line requires 21 days under GMP conditions. Variable costs were estimated at €10,390. The final price for a single CMV-specific T cell line came to €16,000. The final product batch can be split into several doses depending on the final T cell count obtained from expansion and also the design of the treatment strategy. On the other hand, the cost of the antiviral therapy was estimated at €7500 since 900 mg of Valganciclovir cost €75.37 (One Valganciclovir 450 mg box contains 60 film coated tablets and costs €2,261.10). These costs are then multiplied by 100 days which is the duration of treatment. For the 200 days' prophylactic strategy, the cost of the antiviral therapy was estimated at €15000. The GMP cost of a single T cell line was then recalculated if another T cell line was produced in parallel in the same GMP laboratory (two incubators are available in each lab). The GMP fixed costs were estimated at €2,835 for each line. The material and supplies costs were estimated at €6190. The remaining variable costs (€4200) were split between the two cell lines. The final price for a single CMV-specific T cell line came to €11,000.

Variable Resources	Description	Variable costs (€)
Materials and supplies	Media and supplements & Plasticware	5,660
	Reagents for the CliniMacs - PepMix HCMVA (pp65) - PepMix HCMVA (IE-1)	420
	Garments	110 (10 sets)
Personnel	Production personnel	2,200
Utilities	Electricity, water & medical grade gases	350
Maintenance	Corrective maintenance	
Quality Management system	-Depreciation of media-fill, process validation and fees for manufacturing authorization	1,650
	-Cleaning and environmental monitoring	
	Batch Release Testing (testing for sterility, mycoplasma, endotoxin and other items required by the guidelines)	
Total		10,390

Table 15: The variable costs of manufacturing GMP-grade CMV-specific T-cell products. The variable resources of the manufacturing process were identified according to the second level of the CTAT model.

	Unit fixed costs (€)	Unit variable cost (€)	Total unit cost (€)
CMV-specific CTL (1 line/lab)	5,670 (35%)	10,390 (65%)	16,060
CMV-specific CTL (2 lines/lab)	2,835 (25%)	8,290 (75%)	11,125

Table 16: The fixed and variable cost shares in the manufacturing of a single CMV-specific T-cell product. The fixed costs represent 35% while the variable costs represent 65% of the total manufacturing costs. If 2 CMV-specific T-cell products are produced in the same laboratory, the fixed costs represent 25% of the total manufacturing costs.

3.8 Developing New Technologies to Shorten Manufacturing Time: EBV-Specific CTLs

In the case of LCL stimulated T cell lines, two separate GMP manufacturing laboratories are required to avoid cross contamination, one to handle the LCL production and another to perform the T cell expansion. The manufacturing of a single T cell line using this method requires an average of 77 days under GMP conditions. The fixed manufacturing costs were estimated at €30,240 by multiplying the duration of the process by the ADR. Variable costs were estimated at €13,784. The final price for as single EBV-specific LCL stimulated T cell line came to €44,000. However, when using the overlapping peptide-pools method for manufacturing EBV-Specific T cell lines, a single manufacturing laboratory is required. The duration of the process is only 21 days under GMP conditions. As a result, the fixed manufacturing costs were estimated at €5,670 and the variable costs at €11,410 (Table 15, 16). The final price for a single EBV-specific peptide stimulated T cell line came to €17,000 (Figure 9)" (24).

Variable Resources (CTAT Level 2)	Description	Variable costs (€)	
		EBV-specific T-cells (LCL technique)	EBV-specific T-cells (Peptide pool technique)
Materials and supplies	Media and supplements & plasticware	2,200	5,660
	Transfection reagents (EBV supernatant)	550	N/A
	Reagents for the CliniMacs EBV peptide pool	N/A	1,440
	Garments	374 (34 sets)	110 (10 sets)
Personnel	Production personnel	7,800	2,200
Utilities	Electricity, water & medical grade gases	650	350
Maintenance	Corrective maintenance		

Quality Management system	-Depreciation of media-fill, process validation and fees for manufacturing authorization	2,210	1,650
	-Cleaning and environmental monitoring		
	Batch Release Testing (testing for sterility, mycoplasma, endotoxin and other items required by regulation)		
Total		13,784	11,410

Table 17: The variable costs of manufacturing GMP-grade EBV-specific T-cell products. The variable resources of the manufacturing process were identified according to the second level of the CTAT model.

	Unit fixed costs (€)	Unit variable cost (€)	Total unit cost (€)
LCL Technique	30,240 (69%)	13,784 (31%)	44,024
Peptide Pool Technique	5,670 (33%)	11,410 (67%)	17,080

Table 18: The fixed and variable cost shares in the manufacturing of a single EBV-specific T-cell product. The fixed costs of the LCL technique represent 69% while the variable costs represent 31% of the total manufacturing costs. The high percentage of fixed costs is due to the long duration of the manufacturing process. On the other hand, the fixed costs of the peptide pool technique represent only 33% of the total manufacturing costs.

$$\sum_{i=1}^{2} Manufacturing\ costEBV\ (A) = [(€270 \times 77) + (€270 \times 35) + €13,784] = €44,024$$

a) **The total manufacturing costs of a GMP-grade EBV-specific LCL stimulated T cell line.** The duration of manufacturing a single EBV-Specific LCL stimulated T cell line under GMP conditions was estimated at 77 days for one lab and 35 days for the other lab which was then multiplied by the ADR.

$$\sum_{i=1}^{2} Manufacturing\ costEBV\ (B) = [(€270 \times 21) + €11,410] = €17,080$$

b) **The total manufacturing costs of a GMP-grade single EBV-specific peptide stimulated T cell line.** The duration of manufacturing a single EBV-specific peptide stimulated T cell line under GMP conditions was estimated at 21 days which was then multiplied by the ADR.

Figure 10 (A, B): Estimating the manufacturing costs of a single EBV-Specific LCL stimulated T cell product.

Chapter 4: Discussion

CTAT was developed to estimate the GMP facility operating costs associated with the production of cell-based therapies. This model was applied in our newly constructed GMP facility based in Berlin, Germany. For purpose of comparison, a similar CTAT assessment was conducted using an existing GMP facility based at UC Davis, and results were compared to a more standard business cost model that had been used previously. The CTAT model was able to accurately allocate the cost of resources used by the GMP manufacturing process. Identifying the cost drivers of the manufacturing process reveals the key factors that contribute to the rising costs of production. Also, the model focused on the detection and correction of human error during the performance using various quality improvement tools. This will prevent the deviation of actual production levels in comparison with planned schedules. The results also demonstrated the advantage of adopting novel manufacturing technologies that can shorten the duration of production as in the case of EBV-specific CTLs. In particular, there are several benefits from the model which were observed and are summarized under the following points: 1) System cost identification: By using the CTAT model, the organization gains the ability to accurately assess the cost of any given GMP operating system. 2) Project estimates and costing: The model also enables project estimation "as producing a specific unit or product". Through the usage of the fee structure of the facility, a fixed project's cost can be calculated by multiplying the cost element of core processes by the estimated time of use. 3) Optimization and resource planning: Planning and optimizing of GMP operations into the future can be parlayed back into resource requirements by using the SIPOC diagram and the PEC in reverse. 4) Benchmarking: The CTAT model yields a series of values. These values can be used to benchmark the activities of a GMP facility or even a specific product to see where improvements can be made.

4.1 What Makes the CTAT Model Unique?

To the best of our knowledge, no formal analytical system had taken into account the identification of the various tasks required to operate a GMP facility and their associated costs. One of the reasons for this might be the difficulty to separate these tasks from the production process of a GMP-grade product. Therefore, we developed the clean-room technology assessment technique "CTAT" as a two-level assessment model which focuses on the manufacturing process of GMP-grade cell, gene, and tissue therapies. The model was designed as a "standardized structured shell" to be filled according to management objectives in relation to a specific GMP project. "Due to the complicated nature of this process, where resources are not dedicated to only one activity in isolation, the model also aims to analyze and quantify the interdependency that exists between the various activities. For this specific reason, it was designed as a two level model. CTAT attempts to separate out "core" tasks associated with the facility operation from the actual production activities. The model uses a micro-costing approach to measure the manufacturing costs of these therapeutic products. Micro-costing has been reported to be the most appropriate for costing of a novel therapeutic intervention (27). This approach is known to be time consuming due to the level of details required, nevertheless the cost estimates generated by this method have been reported to be accurate and reliable (36). Since it is usually used in the healthcare industry to calculate patient-specific resource use and hospital specific unit costs (36, 37), the method was adjusted to the GMP manufacturing process by acquiring specific cost data. Ideally the CTAT model would be tested prospectively with annual cyclic verification and improvement. However, retrospective application has also shown to be beneficial in validating the predictive accuracy of the model. A flowchart diagram describing the CTAT assessment as being carried out prospectively and retrospectively is shown in figure 2. Following this flowchart will enable other GMP facilities to emulate the model for their own operations"(24).

"Assigning costs to a product should include all costs associated with this product from an organization's value chain. This is a common business practice in the pharmaceutical industry during the pricing of new drugs. The value chain includes activities that range from research and development, through product design and manufacturing to marketing and distribution. However, the non-manufacturing costs are not relevant in academia knowing that R&D is usually financed by grants, and marketing is not a requirement for early phase studies. The first level of the CTAT model represents only the fixed (operating) cost category while the second level represent the variable (production) cost category. Analyzing the operating costs of the Berlin facility prospectively and the California facility retrospectively resulted in significant observations. For instance, although the California facility employs more personnel than the Berlin facility, their costs make up a smaller share of total operating costs. This might be due to the fact that Germany is a very high priced country, particularly when it comes to personnel"(24).

Figure 11: Flowchart diagram describing the components of the CTAT model.

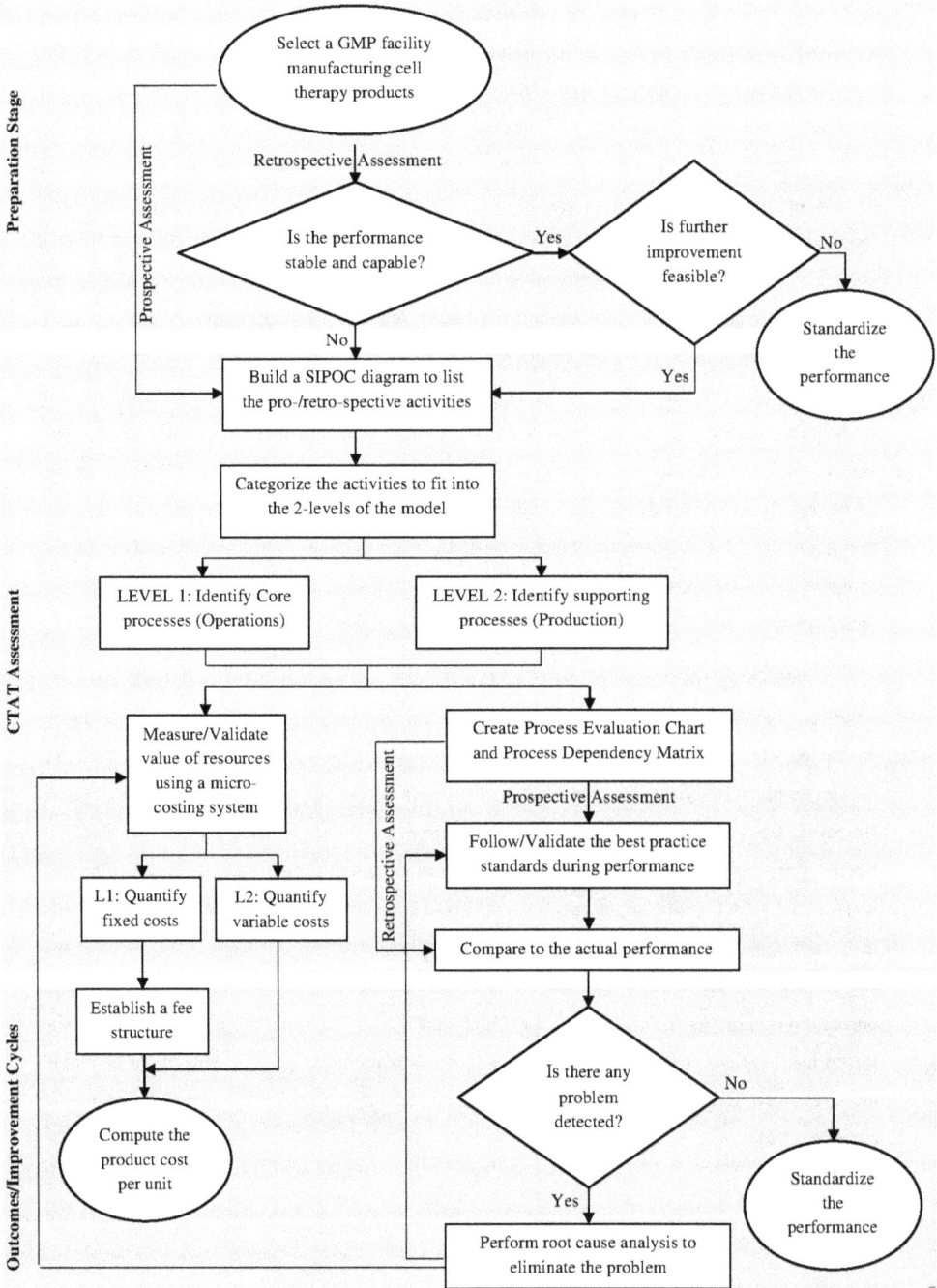

4.2 Significant Differences between the Two Facilities in Terms of Expenses

Interestingly, "the small share of costs for utility consumption in the California facility reflects the significant efforts made by the facility to achieve efficient energy use. To reduce energy costs, in the planning phase the facility already ruled out single pass air, as their experience with previous GMP facilities showed that recirculating air with 60 air changes per hour and 30% bleed in of fresh air and exhaust of used air was appropriate for use in a Class 10,000 manufacturing environment. In addition, highly energy efficient individual small HVAC units were applied to each manufacturing room, effectively creating a so called "split system"; each small air handler only needs to condition a particular small room area, and can be optimally sized for the expected heat load. All HVAC units have variable frequency drives which are programmed to only utilize as much energy as is needed to condition the particular environment. Most of their drives run below 80% nominal energy consumption at all times. The electrical power for the facility and other buildings on the medical campus is created using a natural gas turbine operated by the university. On the other hand, the California facility has identified several processes that could be optimized. For instance, the costs incurred by the QP activities are quite high and can be further reduced if planned properly. The share of costs of the consumable laboratory materials and office supplies is high. This is probably due to the huge size of the facility comprising 6 manufacturing suits and higher number of personnel. Still, there are definitely tangible possibilities to reduce these costs once analyzed" (24).

"From the calculated annual expenses, an ADR (assumes no profit) fee structure was calculated for the Berlin facility at €270. This ADR can be used to assign appropriate facility-use charges associated with specific cell therapy product manufacturing activities. Since the capacity utilization based on the facility demands is expected to be low, the daily rate was more suitable and applicable. For a facility to use an ADR, capacity utilization should be based upon the maximum production rate of this facility. As an example, let's assume that we are producing a cell product every 3 weeks. Factoring in the time needed for change-over procedures (cleaning and disinfection after each production cycle), the maximum rate of production is expected to be 15 batches per year. In case one of the labs is not being used, then some of the running GMP costs will not be reimbursed. Thus, if academic facilities use an ADR, this rate should be re-evaluated every year according to the research projects supported by the facility" (24).

"The California facility had already an AHR in place. Although the rate itself is not set out to generate profit, the facility management needs to turn a "profit" from their operations. The reason is that the rate was designed to cover the expenses of other manufacturing rooms while they are not being used. It was also set to cover the GMP facility costs over a period of 3 years without having to change the rate and go through the rates committee again. Additionally, the rate was designed to cover the expenses of raises to be given to personnel, and to cover unforeseen issues, such as equipment having to be repaired or replaced. When the facility quotes a price for GMP manufacturing, the customers will only be charged for time requiring the presence of a production personnel (long incubation periods are then excluded). In addition to this rate the facility also needs to charge the cost for reagents needed for each particular product. Following the retrospective CTAT assessment, the UC Davis observed processes consuming more resources than expected and identified hidden costs that were not previously addressed within their already existing business model as discussed in section 3.5. Therefore, they calculated these costs and considered adjusting the hourly rate in the next cycle, when the rate will be re-negotiated"(24).

4.3   GMP Manufacturing Activities are Complex and Interdependent

"Given the complexity and interdependence of GMP manufacturing activities, it is frequently difficult to plan a project in such a way as to efficiently balance the load across all resources"(24). For example during a period of no production, some resources such as personnel must remain available to maintain the controlled environment. When a manufacturing process begins, enough personnel need to be available to immediately handle the additional work load of product manufacturing. However, it is not considered a legitimate charge for a GMP manufacturing project to bear the cost of a resource that has to be available and needs to be maintained during non-manufacturing times. This fact remains one of the major financial hurdles facing GMP facilities in academia with limited budget and small-scale production. "However, an approach which is feasible in academia can be employed by sharing resources across multiple new projects whenever possible. This will minimize the amount of time at which the resource is not being productive. Another approach is to plan and optimize the performance of the different activities probably. This was the purpose of integrating the PEC tool in our model. The PEC assisted the California facility in identifying several defects in the management of the manufacturing processes. As a result, the facility is currently developing best practice standards and conducting RCA to correct these defects and reduce costs"(24).

4.4 CTAT Model is a Better Predictor of Financial Performance than Business Models

Even though the concept of a business model is potentially relevant to all pharmaceutical companies, only few publications exist that assess the applicability of business models in the pharmaceutical manufacturing sector (38). However, our search found a substantial amount of literature discussing the concept of business models mostly in e-business (39–42) but with varying perspectives, strategies, value configurations and components. As a result, no generally accepted definition of a business model exists. The results of the CTAT and the business model, both were tested in the California-based facility, show several key differences. The business models can unintentionally allocate a disproportionate share of "indirect" or "fixed" costs among the facility's operations. Also it can overlook other costs that are more specific to the GMP manufacturing process. The process was seen to absorb valuable resources with their value becoming sunk costs since they are unrecoverable at that time point. The interrelation between uncertainty and sunk costs is the best explanation for this issue, since the business model provided limited information regarding GMP operations and product manufacturing. Additionally, production optimization is achieved only via business decisions such as negotiating contracts and seeking suitable vendors. However due to the data requirements of the CTAT model (Figure 11) which is based on a common GMP terminology and its integrated optimization tools, chances to improve the performance of a GMP facility are quite high. This detailed structure also benefits the allocation of costs that can be traced directly and accurately to a specific activity using the micro-costing system. CTAT evaluates the impact of a change in any cost driver on the manufacturing process by identifying its fixed and variable resources. Categorizing the costs into fixed and variable ones in the CTAT model allows an accurate allocation of expenses. Additionally, it facilitates cost-volume-profit analysis and the determining of the break-even-point of the manufacturing process, since a contribution margin can be calculated. To further understand the differences between CTAT and business models, we explored their characteristics in Table 3.

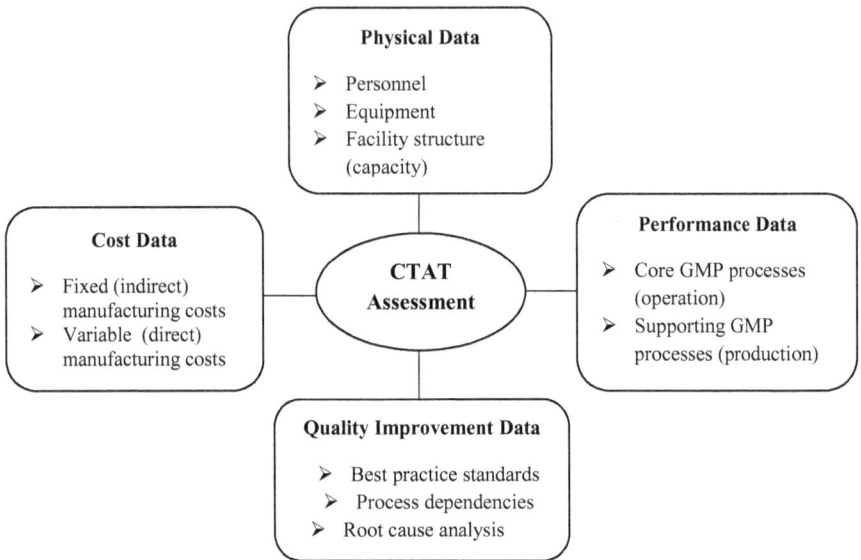

Figure 12: The data requirements for carrying out the CTAT assessment. These different data influence the manufacturing process of cell therapy products. The physical and performance data could be seen as the key factors in the early stage of the assessment. Quality improvement data is highly subjective and influenced by management decisions. Cost data are most essential for CTAT assessment. However, cost data is dependent on the accuracy of the cost breakdown structure.

	Business Model	CTAT Model
Definition	Various definitions exist, however the earliest (39) describes the business model as: architecture for the product, service, and information flows; the potential benefits for the business actors; and the sources of revenues.	It is an operational framework that describes the logic and activities of GMP facilities manufacturing medicinal products within a coupled efficient performance/financial micro-estimation approach in order to create an optimized economic value for these products.
Significance	Act as a management plan for profit-oriented organization aiming at cost recovery, revenue generation and securing sources of funding (43).	Offers a concise representation of the interdependent operational relationships while exploring opportunities for improvement through generating an inclusive database of information on cost

		and performance.
Components	The structure of business models is ambiguous. One study (44) identifies four key components: 1) customer value proposition, 2) profit formula, 3) key resources 4) key processes.	The structured framework is based on two levels: operational level and production level. Both levels list all the activities with strong correlation to the manufacturing process.
Adoptability	There exists no insight on how to design individual components depending on specific industry settings (in-flexible) (45).	The model is designed as a standardized shell in accordance to the GMP manufacturing process that can be adopted by different facilities and for different products.
Consistency	The nature and causality of relationships among business model components are not well defined (45).	The relationship among the components of the model is well defined in a dependency matrix.
Applicability	Most of the existing concepts of business models are developed from theory (45).	The CTAT model is empirically constructed in accordance to the GMP manufacturing process.
Feasibility	Requires extensive managing skills	Can be carried out easily by the GMP facility management.

Table 19: Comparison between the conventional business models and the CTAT model. The business model might be unable to effectively measure the costs of manufacturing GMP-grade cell-based products due to possible three reasons. The first reason could be structural uncertainty; the model may have a structure which makes it impossible to truly describe the GMP activities. This is probably due to the fact that business models follow a strict protocol, which is difficult to be adjusted to the GMP manufacturing technology. A second reason could be measurement uncertainty; projections and estimates contained in the model may differ greatly from the actual performance. A third reason could be lack of informative data; the data may be insufficient to fully describe the parameters of the model. In practice, all of these factors are usually present to some extent.

4.5   Key Cost Drivers that Contribute to the Rising Costs of Production

To understand the impact of using a fee structure on estimating COGs, the relation between cost and cost driver has to be examined in greater details. A cost driver is a factor that causes variations in a cost. The relevant manufacturing costs of cellular products can be broken down into fixed and variable costs. The product's "validation and media fill", "direct material" and "direct personnel" are examples of direct costs and have a variable cost share that depends on the volume of the production. The operations which are needed to maintain the GMP status of the facility e.g. "qualification program", "preventive maintenance", and "environmental monitoring" are examples of indirect costs and have a fixed cost share because they are independent of the actual utilization times. For the total variable costs per year, the cost driver is the number of production cycles that are carried out in the facility. However, for the total fixed costs per year the cost drivers are the size of the GMP facility, personnel wages and the degree of optimization of the processes design. On the other hand, for the unit fixed cost (fixed costs contributing to the cost of a single cell line), the only cost drivers is time or in other words the duration of the manufacturing process. Increasing the duration of the product manufacturing would result in a linear increase in the fixed costs. For products that need less time for production, the variable costs will then have the dominant share of costs. This relation has been shown in the case of shifting from the LCL technique to the peptide pool technique for the manufacturing of EBV-specific CTLs. The use of the LCL approach in a GMP setting is financially problematic due to the long culture times needed for cell expansion. Additionally, this expansion method may also be impractical for larger clinical trials where the manufacturing of large numbers of patient-specific products and rapid infusion of cells are required. The cost of cell maintenance in GMP grade culture conditions for an extended period of time is the main factor that greatly influences the cell production costs.

4.6   The Relation between Manufacturing Costs and Production Capacity

Another cost driver for profit generation is the scale of the production. As a result, our research in estimating the manufacturing expenses of cell-based products was greatly motivated by the relation of pricing decisions to capacities of production. In most of the cost modeling efforts, capacity constraints are ignored and production costs are assumed to be linear, thereby limiting the degree to which costs are realistic. One reason why capacity constraints have been ignored is that accounting for production scale economies can significantly complicate the pricing process. Usually, calculating the production capacity of a manufacturing facility should be based on a supply/demand relationship. Scaling up production levels obviously reduces GMP fixed costs. One way to achieve efficiency of scale, high-throughput production by parallel processing of multiple, separate products in one GMP manufacturing suite could be considered. In this case, two sets of incubators are necessary for incubating each product separately. We observed from the cost-minimization study that the production costs will decrease by 30% for each T-cell line if two cell lines are produced in parallel in a single lab. This relation between scaling up production and reduction of costs is further explained in a hypothetical break-even point analysis for the Berlin facility (Figure 12). Another observation from the cost minimization study is that immunotherapy in comparison with standard of care may offer significant advantages to the healthcare systems by bringing additional clinical benefit at a reasonable extra cost.

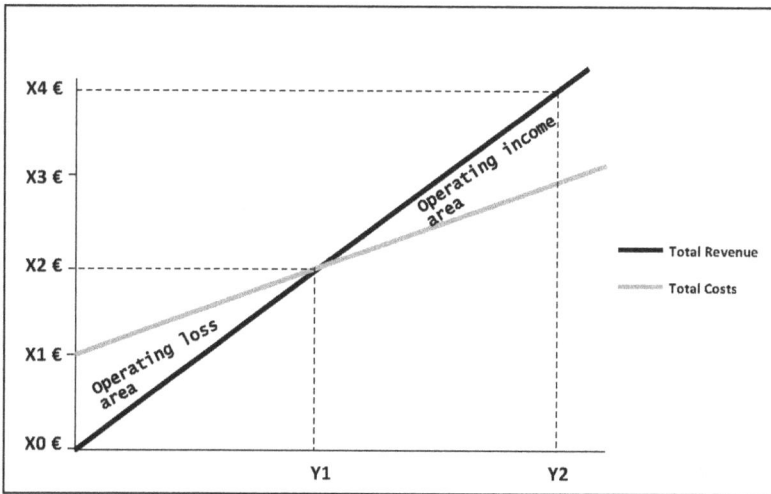

Figure 13: A hypothetical break-even analysis of manufacturing GMP-grade Cell therapy products. The figure presents a cost-volume-profit graph for GMP grade cell lines. Notice that when no cells are produced, fixed costs are X1 €, resulting in a loss of 100% of these costs per year. As manufacturing volume increases, the loss decreases by the contribution margin for each cell line produced. The cost and revenue lines intersect at the break-even point of Y1 lines, which means zero loss and zero profit (fixed and variable costs are covered). Then, as manufacturing increase beyond this break-even point, we see an increase in income. The unit contribution of fixed costs decreases by half (X4 €) when the production volume reaches Y2 lines. This can be achieved by producing two parallel cell lines in one manufacturing laboratory using two separate incubators.

Chapter 5: Conclusion and Outlook

The novel CTAT model, which we tested on two GMP facilities in a prospective and retrospective manner, has shown several benefits. The model was able to allocate accurately the cost of resources used by the GMP manufacturing process. Also, the model focused on the detection and correction of human error using various quality improvement tools. Finally, the model fulfilled its main purpose through the accurate estimation of product costs for two different GMP-grade cellular products. CTAT has shown that the production costs of cell therapies are mainly dependent on the method, duration and capacity of production. The share of fixed operating costs in the final product can act as an indicator for the efficiency of production. Although scaling up manufacturing can also reduce fixed costs, financial decisions for adding production capacity (for instance, hiring extra staff or purchasing extra equipment) requires proper planning. This strategy can be useful for pharmaceutical companies which are keen on developing a process that is economically adaptable to mass production. However, this should also be paired with developing effective marketing approaches; otherwise the product may not be commercially viable.

In contrast to the pharmaceutical industry, academic institutions usually have low production capacity serving specific non-for profit purposes. Therefore, developing new technologies that can shorten the duration of production while optimizing performance are probably the main way of reducing costs. This was demonstrated in the manufacturing of EBV-specific CTLs, where a new method of producing EBV-specific T-cell lines was developed. Currently the generation of these products requires EBV-infected B-cells (LCL). This technique could be successfully replaced by chemically synthesizable EBV peptide-pools. As a result, the production time was shortened significantly (from 77 to 21 days) and has reached a higher level of biosafety. This kind of knowledge is becoming a key component of the academic translational science infrastructure especially with the current focus on optimizing costs of cell-based therapies. Despite all these efforts, the major disadvantages of manufacturing cell therapeutic products in academia will be the small-scale production, expensive asset base (partially related to less-optimized process design) and significantly high personnel costs.

Current progress and future prospects:

We believe, as we concluded at the end of our study, that the translation of the currently expensive process of manufacturing GMP grade cell-based products into clinically practice could greatly benefit from the application of the CTAT model. We are currently using the results of the CTAT model for the purpose of applying for a NUB status as a step toward the reimbursement of these innovative therapies. We are also planning to validate the performance of the model on an annual basis in our GMP facility. This will enable us to further develop optimization tools to reduce production costs. Since we are a translational center, the results of the model will be used to perform an accurate cost-effectiveness analysis during and after the clinical development phase of these therapies. The model can be a good candidate to be transformed into an appropriate electronic format to widen and facilitate future application. The model can also be a tool to strengthen the collaboration between the industry and academia with both benefiting from each other's experiences.

List of References

1. Schneider, C. K., P. Salmikangas, B. Jilma, *et.al*. 2010. Challenges with advanced therapy medicinal products and how to meet them. *Nature reviews. Drug discovery* 9: 195–201.

2. Belardelli, F., P. Rizza, F. Moretti, C. Carella, M. C. Galli, and G. Migliaccio. 2011. Translational research on advanced therapies. *Annali dell'Istituto superiore di sanità* 47: 72–8.

3. Brestrich, G., S. Zwinger, A. Roemhild, M. Noutsias, M. Rohde, K. Keeren, B. Sawitzki, H.-D. Volk, P. Reinke, and M. H. Hammer. Generation of HCMV-specific T-cell lines from seropositive solid-organ-transplant recipients for adoptive T-cell therapy. *Journal of immunotherapy (Hagerstown, Md.: 1997)* 32: 932–40.

4. Hammer, M. H., G. Brestrich, A. Mittenzweig, A. Roemhild, S. Zwinger, M. Subklewe, C. Beier, A. Kurtz, N. Babel, H.-D. Volk, and P. Reinke. Generation of EBV-specific T cells for adoptive immunotherapy: a novel protocol using formalin-fixed stimulator cells to increase biosafety. *Journal of immunotherapy (Hagerstown, Md.: 1997)* 30: 817–24.

5. Buckley, R. H. 2011. Transplantation of hematopoietic stem cells in human severe combined immunodeficiency: longterm outcomes. *Immunologic research* 49: 25–43.

6. Fischer, A., S. Hacein-Bey-Abina, and M. Cavazzana-Calvo. 2011. Gene therapy for primary adaptive immune deficiencies. *The Journal of allergy and clinical immunology* 127: 1356–9.

7. Rayment, E. A., and D. J. Williams. 2010. Concise review: mind the gap: challenges in characterizing and quantifying cell- and tissue-based therapies for clinical translation. *Stem cells (Dayton, Ohio)* 28: 996–1004.

8. Martín, P. G., A. R. Martinez, V. G. Lara, and B. C. Naveros. 2012. Regulatory considerations in production of a cell therapy medicinal product in Europe to clinical research. *Clinical and experimental medicine* .

9. Smith, D. 2010. Commercialization challenges associated with induced pluripotent stem cell-based products. *Regenerative medicine* 5: 593–603.

10. McAllister, T. N., N. Dusserre, M. Maruszewski, and N. L'heureux. 2008. Cell-based therapeutics from an economic perspective: primed for a commercial success or a research sinkhole? *Regenerative medicine* 3: 925–37.

11. Commission directive 2003/94/EC of 8 October 2003 laying down the principles and guidelines of good manufacturing practice in respect of medicinal products for human use and investigational medicinal products for human use. *Official J Eur Union* 22–26.

12. EudraLex—EU GMP Volume 4 (2009) Good manufacturing practice (GMP) guidelines-annex 1: manufacture of sterile medicinal products.EU GMP-Annex 1: Manufacture of Sterile Medicinal Products.

13. CFR—Code of Federal Regulations Title 21, Part 211. Current good manufacturing practice for finished pharmaceuticals.

14. Rossig, C. 2012. Anti-tumor cytotoxic T lymphocytes targeting solid tumors: ready for clinical trials. *Cytotherapy* 14: 4–6.

15. Stroncek, D., D. Berlyne, B. Fox, A. Gee, S. Heimfeld, R. Lindblad, K. Loper, D. McKenna, C. Rooney, M. Sabatino, E. Wagner, T. Whiteside, D. Wood, and T. Heath-Mondoro. 2010. Developments in clinical cell therapy. *Cytotherapy* 12: 425–8.

16. Moos, W. H., and K. Kodukula. 2011. Nonprofit pharma: solutions to what ails the industry. *Current medicinal chemistry* 18: 3437–40.

17. D, J. 2012. mall–Batch-Size Production: Addressing the Commercial Challenge. *BioProcess International* 10.

18. H, C. 2005. Open innovation: A new paradigm for understanding industrial innovation. .

19. Singh, A. R., and S. A. Singh. 2007. Guidelines, editors, pharma and the biological paradigm shift. *Mens sana monographs* 5: 27–30.

20. Drummond, M., B. Jönsson, F. Rutten, and T. Stargardt. 2011. Reimbursement of pharmaceuticals: reference pricing versus health technology assessment. *The European journal of health economics : HEPAC: health economics in prevention and care* 12: 263–71.

21. Gerber, A., S. Stock, and C.-M. Dintsios. 2011. Reflections on the changing face of German pharmaceutical policy: how far is Germany from value-based pricing? *PharmacoEconomics* 29: 549–53.

22. Brechmann, T., and W. Schmiegel. 2007. [Procedure of implementation of new methods of examination and treatment in the G-DRG system (NUB procedure)]. *Medizinische Klinik (Munich, Germany: 1983)* 102: 683–4.

23. Rowley JA. Developing Cell Therapy Biomanufacturing Processes. Chem. Eng. Progr. 2010 Nov; 106(11):50–55.

24. Abou-El-Enein, M., A. Römhild, D. Kaiser, C. Beier, G. Bauer, H.-D. Volk, and P. Reinke. 2013. Good Manufacturing Practices (GMP) manufacturing of advanced therapy medicinal products: a novel tailored model for optimizing performance and estimating costs. *Cytotherapy* 15: 362–383.

25. Taitz, J., K. Genn, V. Brooks, D. Ross, K. Ryan, B. Shumack, T. Burrell, and P. Kennedy. 2010. System-wide learning from root cause analysis: a report from the New South Wales Root Cause Analysis Review Committee. *Quality & safety in health care* 19: e63.

26. Yassine, A. A. 2004. An Introduction to Modeling and Analyzing Complex Product Development Processes Using the Design Structure Matrix (DSM) Method. *Product Development Research Laboratory. University of Illinois* 1–17.

27. Barnett, P. G. 2009. An improved set of standards for finding cost for cost-effectiveness analysis. *Medical care* 47: S82–8.

28. Higgins, A. M., and A. H. Harris. 2012. Health economic methods: cost-minimization, cost-effectiveness, cost-utility, and cost-benefit evaluations. *Critical care clinics* 28: 11–24, v.

29. Kotton, C. N., D. Kumar, A. M. Caliendo, A. Asberg, S. Chou, D. R. Snydman, U. Allen, and A. Humar. 2010. International consensus guidelines on the management of cytomegalovirus in solid organ transplantation. *Transplantation* 89: 779–95.

30. *ROTE LISTE® Buch, Einzelausgabe: ISBN 978-3-939192-50-3, Rote Liste® Service GmbH,*.

67

31. Rerolle, J.-P., J.-C. Szelag, and Y. Le Meur. 2007. Unexpected rate of severe leucopenia with the association of mycophenolate mofetil and valganciclovir in kidney transplant recipients. *Nephrology, dialysis, transplantation: official publication of the European Dialysis and Transplant Association - European Renal Association* 22: 671–2.

32. Brestrich, G., S. Zwinger, A. Fischer, M. Schmück, A. Röhmhild, M. H. Hammer, A. Kurtz, L. Uharek, C. Knosalla, H. Lehmkuhl, H.-D. Volk, and P. Reinke. 2009. Adoptive T-cell therapy of a lung transplanted patient with severe CMV disease and resistance to antiviral therapy. *American journal of transplantation: official journal of the American Society of Transplantation and the American Society of Transplant Surgeons* 9: 1679–84.

33. Hammer, M. H., S. Meyer, G. Brestrich, A. Moosmann, F. Kern, L. Tesfa, N. Babel, A. Mittenzweig, C. M. Rooney, W. Hammerschmidt, H.-D. Volk, and P. Reinke. 2005. HLA type-independent generation of antigen-specific T cells for adoptive immunotherapy. *European journal of immunology* 35: 2250–8.

34. Giordano, R., L. Lazzari, and P. Rebulla. 2004. Clinical grade cell manipulation. *Vox sanguinis* 87: 65–72.

35. Neschadim, A., J. A. McCart, A. Keating, and J. A. Medin. 2007. A roadmap to safe, efficient, and stable lentivirus-mediated gene therapy with hematopoietic cell transplantation. *Biology of blood and marrow transplantation: journal of the American Society for Blood and Marrow Transplantation* 13: 1407–16.

36. Riewpaiboon, A., S. Malaroje, and S. Kongsawatt. 2007. Effect of costing methods on unit cost of hospital medical services. *Tropical medicine & international health: TM & IH* 12: 554–63.

37. Reed, S. D., J. Y. Friedman, A. Gnanasakthy, and K. A. Schulman. 2003. Comparison of hospital costing methods in an economic evaluation of a multinational clinical trial. *International journal of technology assessment in health care* 19: 396–406.

38. Rasmussen B. Aspects of the Pharmaceutical Business Model: Implications for Australia. Pharmaceutical Industry Project Working Paper No.15. 2003. CSES, Victoria University, Melbourne.

39. Timmers P.Business Models for Electronic Markets. Electronic Markets. 1998;8(2):3-8.

40. Amit R, Zott C. Value creation in e-business. Strategic Management Journal. 2001;22(6-7): 493-520.

41. Petrovic O , Kittl C, & Teksten RD. Developing Business Models for E-Business, International Conference on Electronic Commerce. 2001. Munich, Germany.

42. Dubosson-Torbay M, Osterwalder A, Pigneur Y. E-Business Model Design, Classification, and Measurements. Thunderbird International Business Review. 2002;44(1): 5-23.

43. Feng HY, Froud J, Johal S, Haslam C, Williams K. A new business model? The capital market and the new economy. Economy and Society. 2001;30(4): 467-503.

44. Johnson MW, Christensen CM, Kagermann H. Reinventing Your Business Model. Harvard Business Review. 2008;86(12):50.

45. Klang D, Wallnöfer M, Hacklin F. The anatomy of the business model: a syntactical review and research agenda. In: DRUID summer conference on "Opening Up Innovation: Strategy, Organization and Technology", Imperial College London Business School, UK, June 2010.

Dedication

This work is dedicated to my wonderful and loving family. I honor the memory of my dad, the late Samir Abou-El-Enein, who departed this life July 29th, 2010. I honor the memory of my mom, the late Nadra Fayad who passed away July 8th, 1990. The greatest impact my parents has had on my life is their legacy of hard work and an honest life. They have always stressed the importance of education throughout my life and have been my strongest source of encouragement and support of my endeavors. This dissertation is dedicated to my beloved sister Rehab, who is my constant source of determination and gives me the will to succeed and to my brothers Ahmed and Ramy for their love and constant encouragement. To my nieces Salma and Hannah who inspire me each day of my life. To my extended family and my many friends, thank you for all the love, support and encouragement.

Acknowledgements

It is with great pleasure that I thank those who made this work possible. I sincerely thank Prof. Dr. Petra Reinke, my first supervisor for her outstanding guidance over the years. I admire her drive, hard-work and willingness to train and impart knowledge to her students. I sincerely appreciate Prof. Dr. Hans-Dieter Volk, my second supervisor for his scientific insights and valuable comments during our group meetings. I sincerely thank Daniel Kaiser, my mentor for his outstanding mentorship, friendship and valuable contribution to my dissertation research. I extend my sincere gratitude to Andy Römhild and Carola Beier for their time and valuable input to the progress of this research. I extend my heartfelt thanks to Prof. Gerhard Bauer, University of California UC Davis, for being instrumental in establishing data collections used in this work. Finally, I acknowledge my many colleagues for their many acts of kindness and listening ears during the many good and few bad times.